COZY COTTAGECORE
COLORING BOOK FOR ADULTS

ANTI-STRESS, ANXIETY, AND RELAXATION
COLORING BOOK WITH VINTAGE
COUNTRYSIDE COTTAGES, WILDFLOWER
AND MORE

This Book Belongs To:

....

....

COLOR TEST AREA

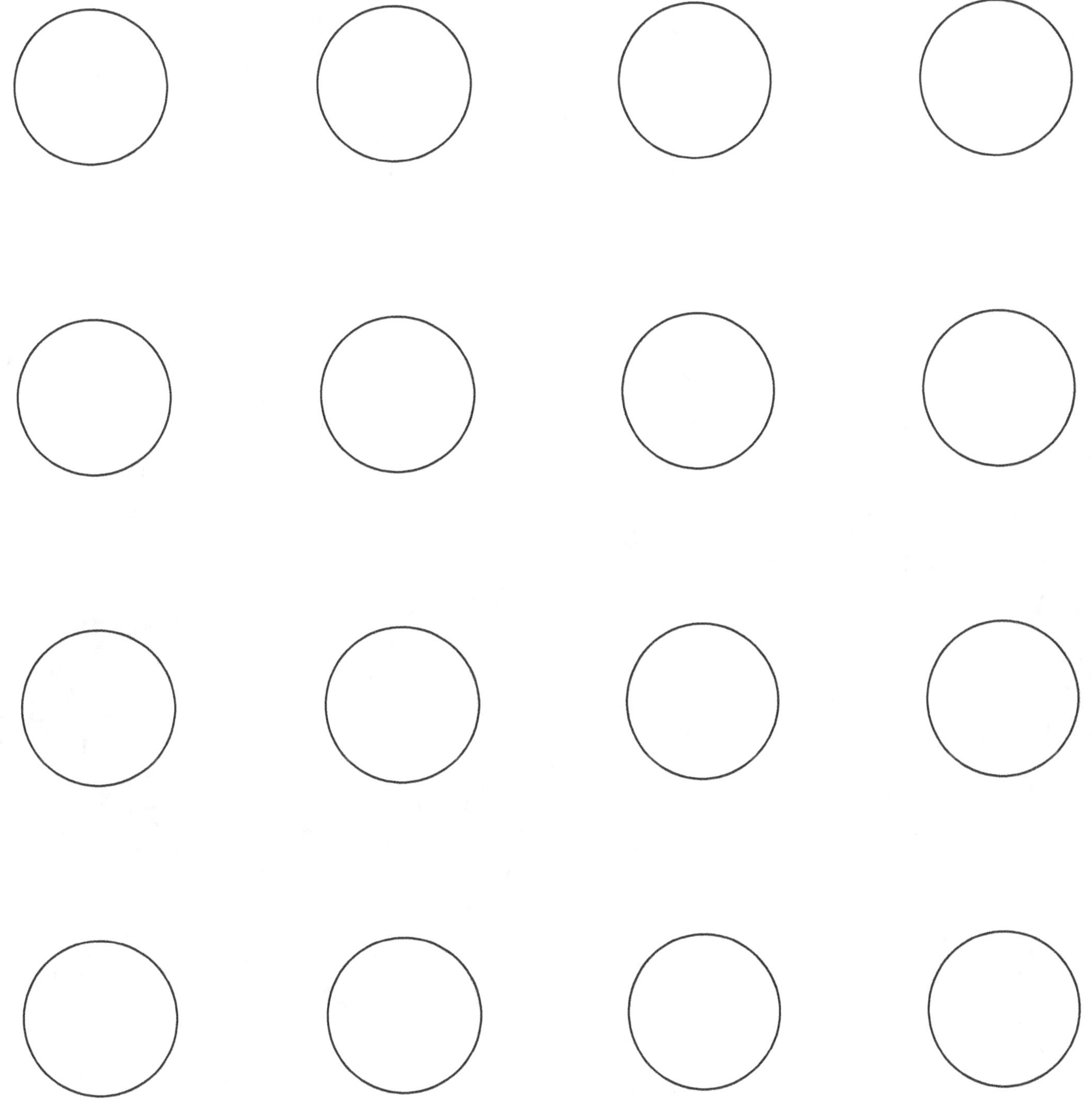

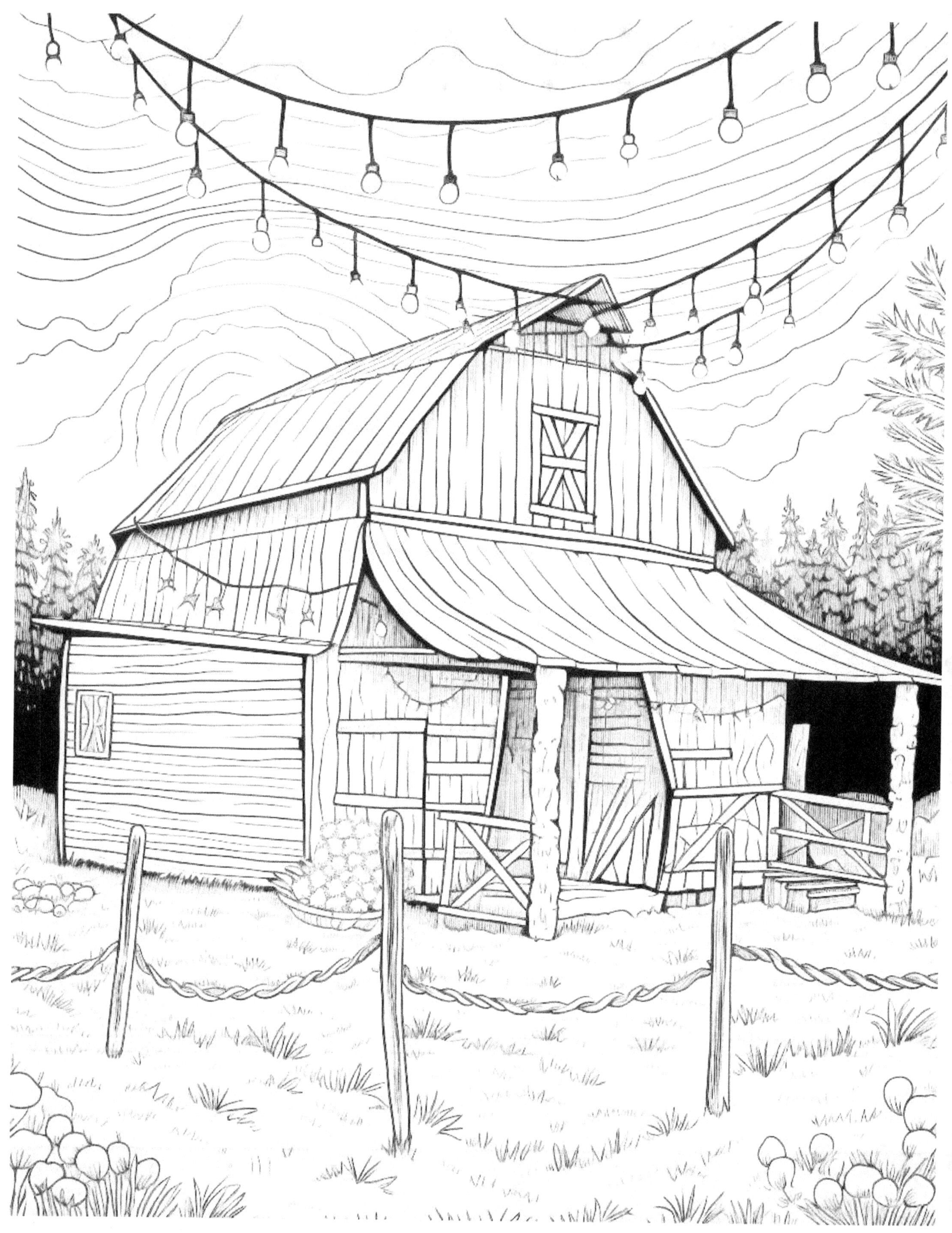

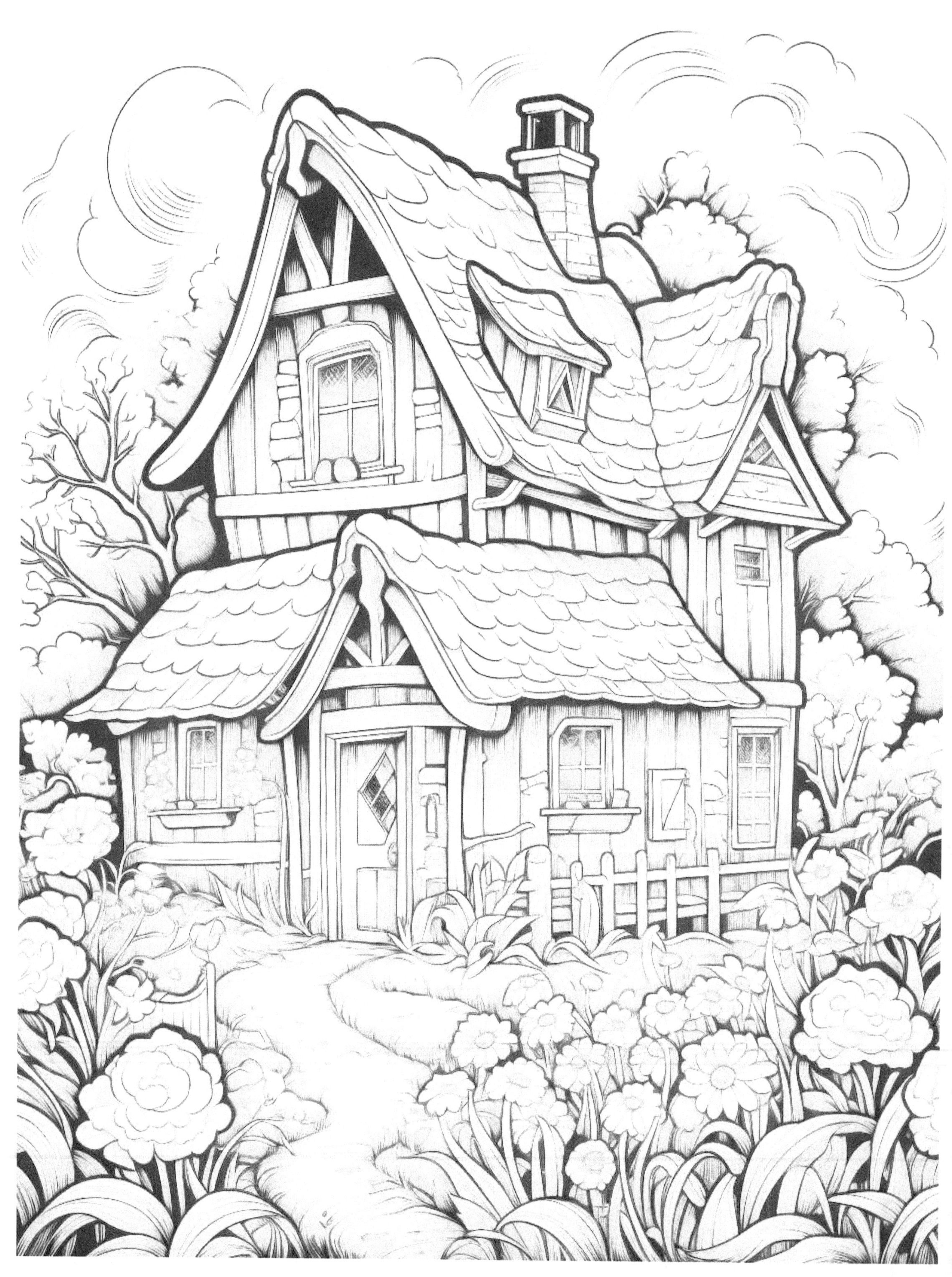

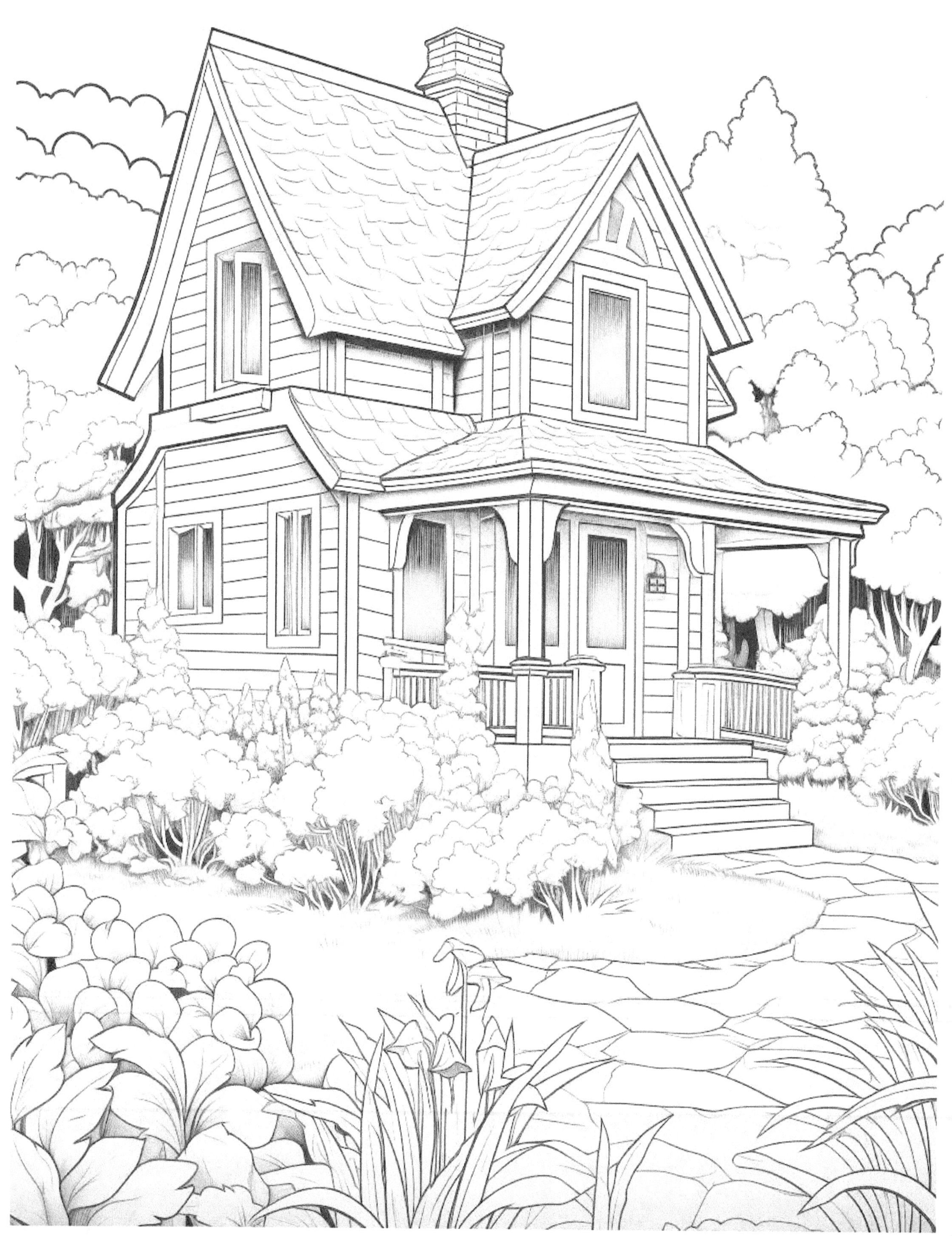

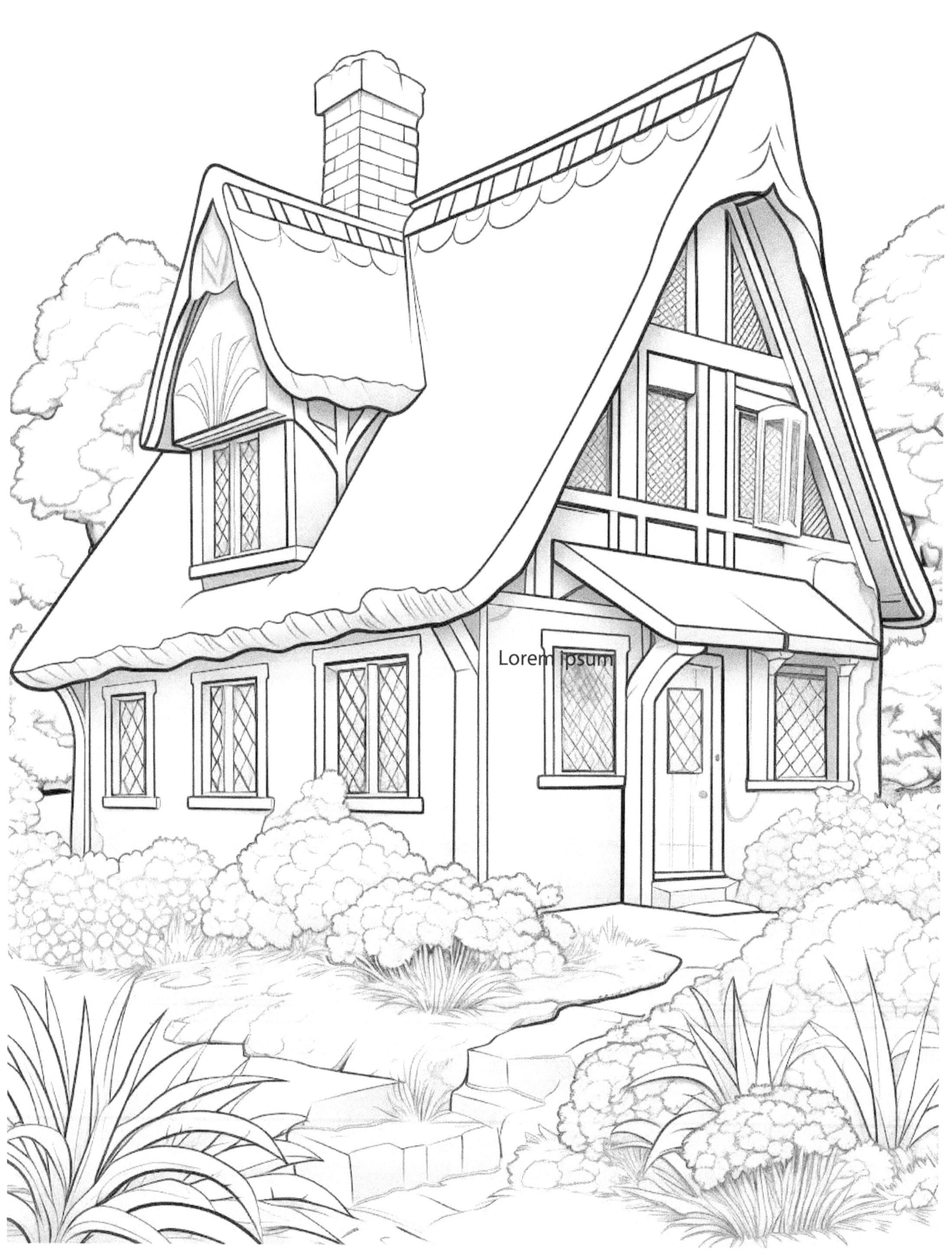
Lorem ipsum

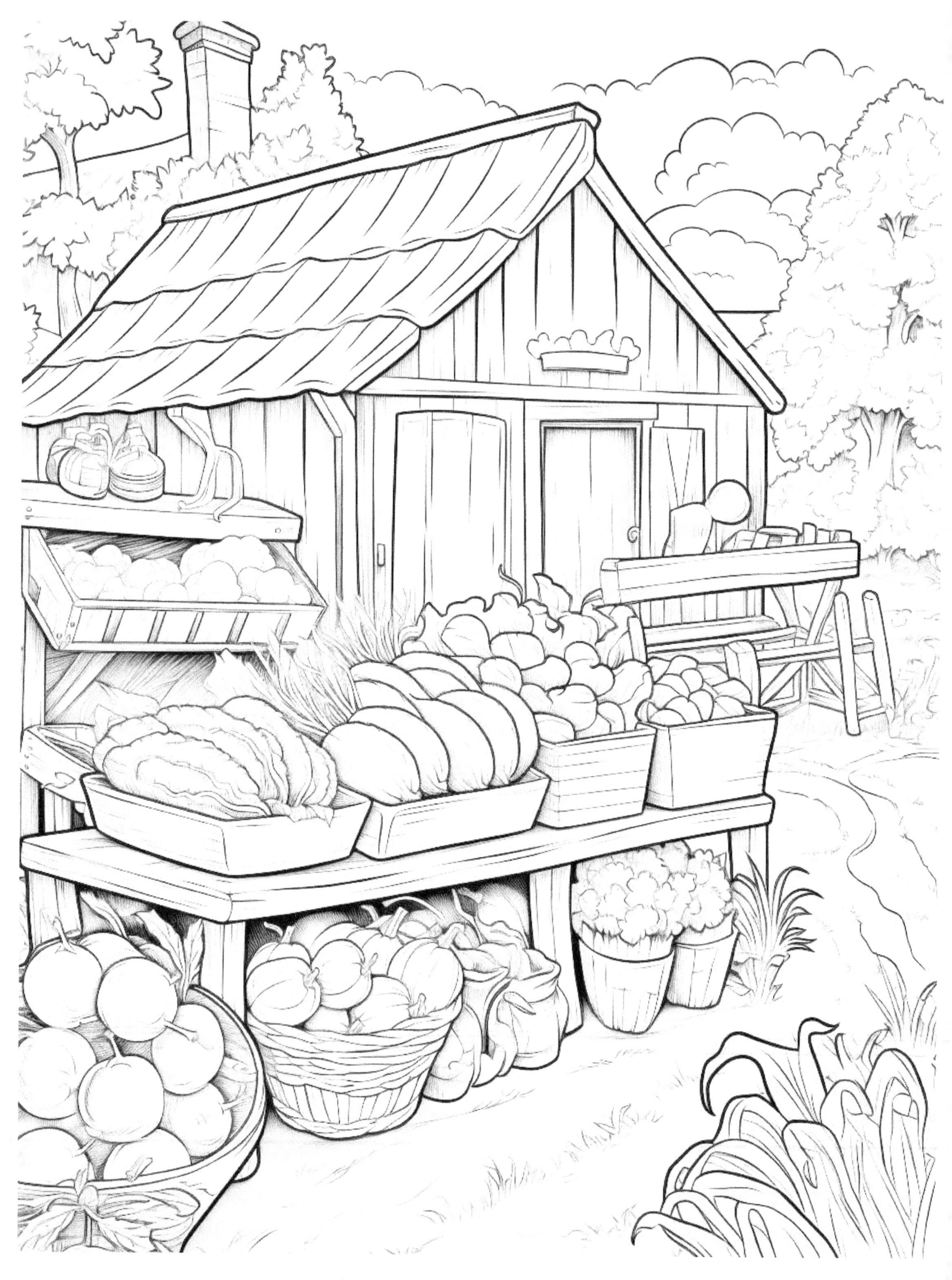

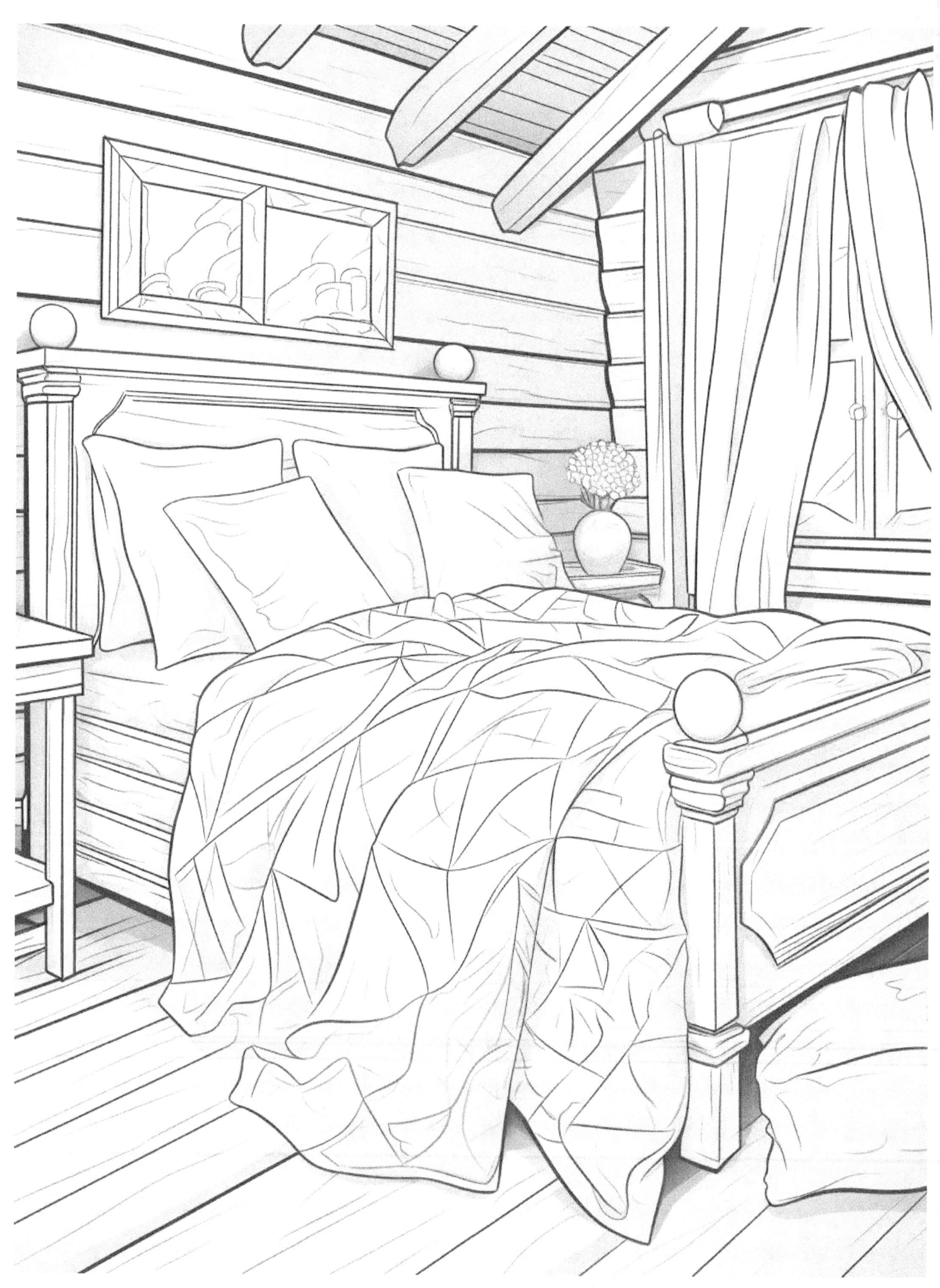

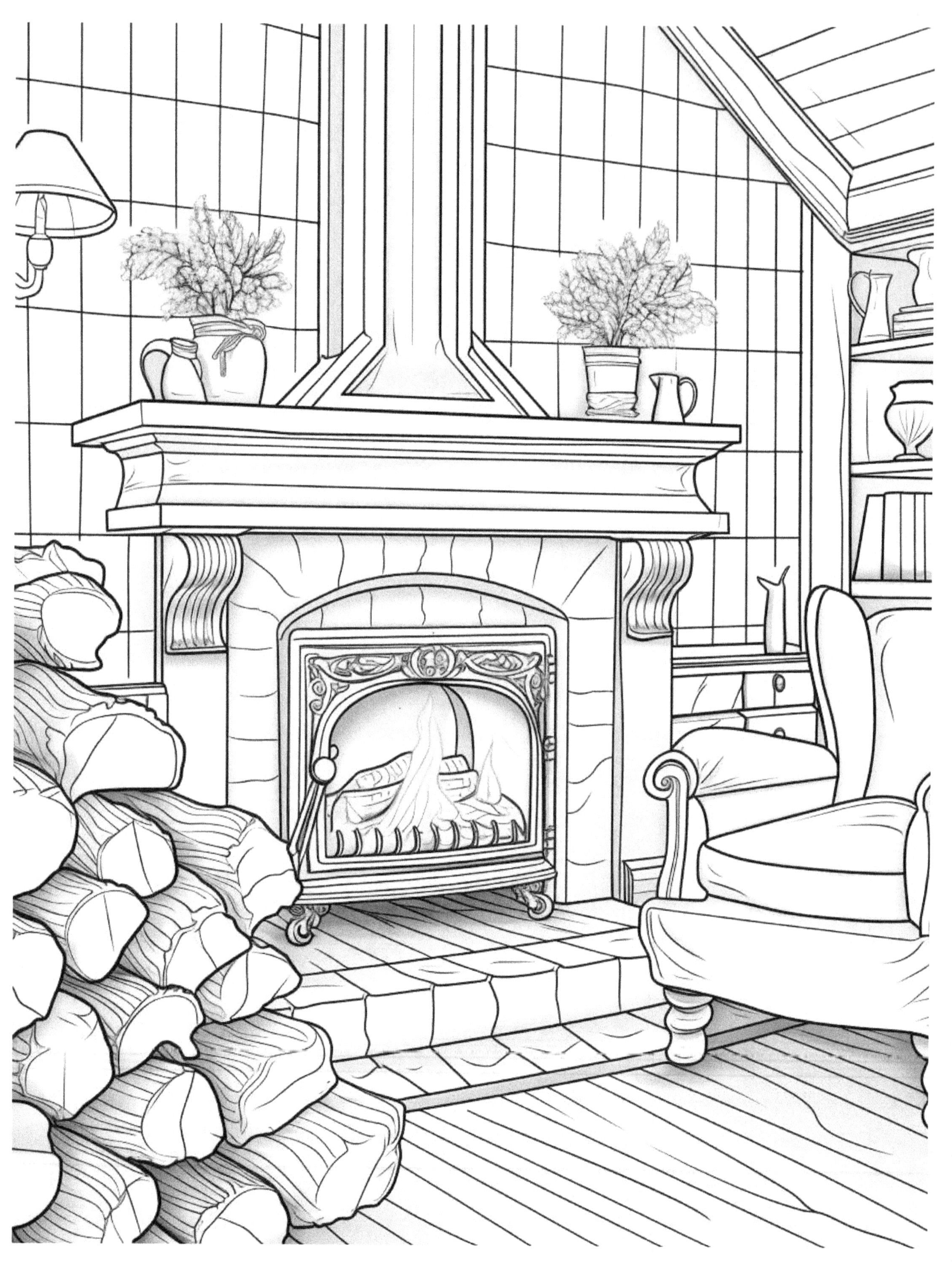

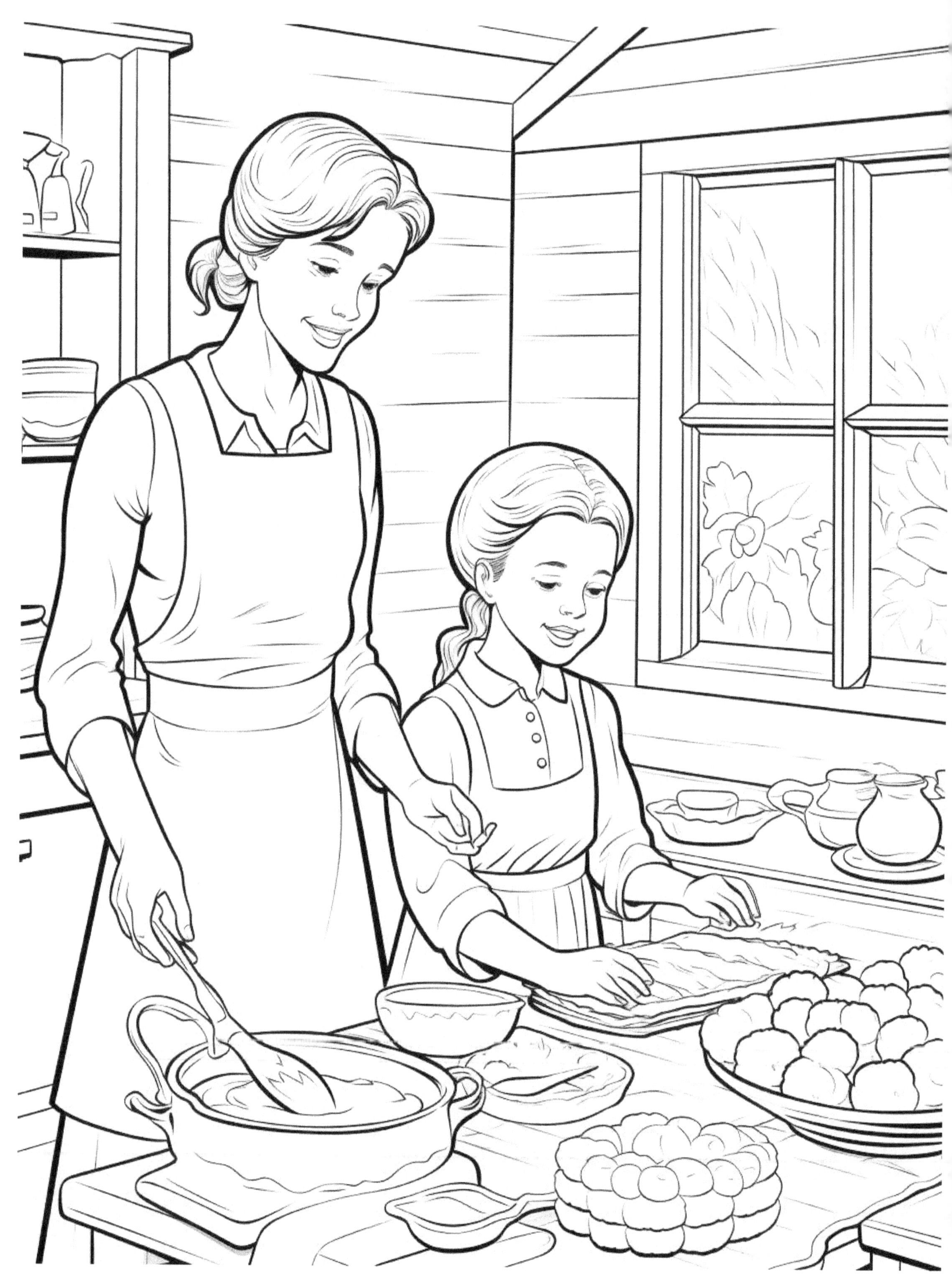

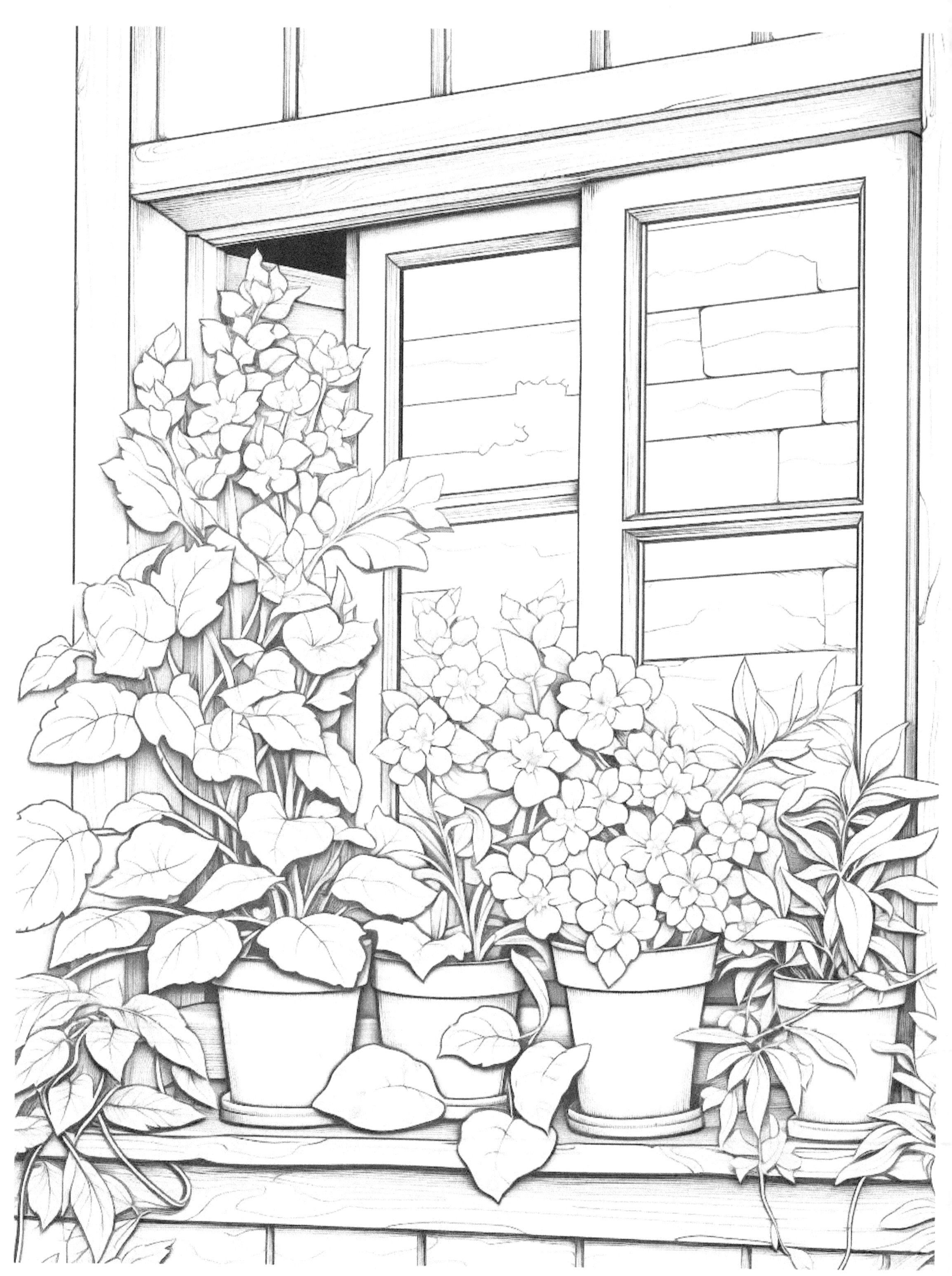

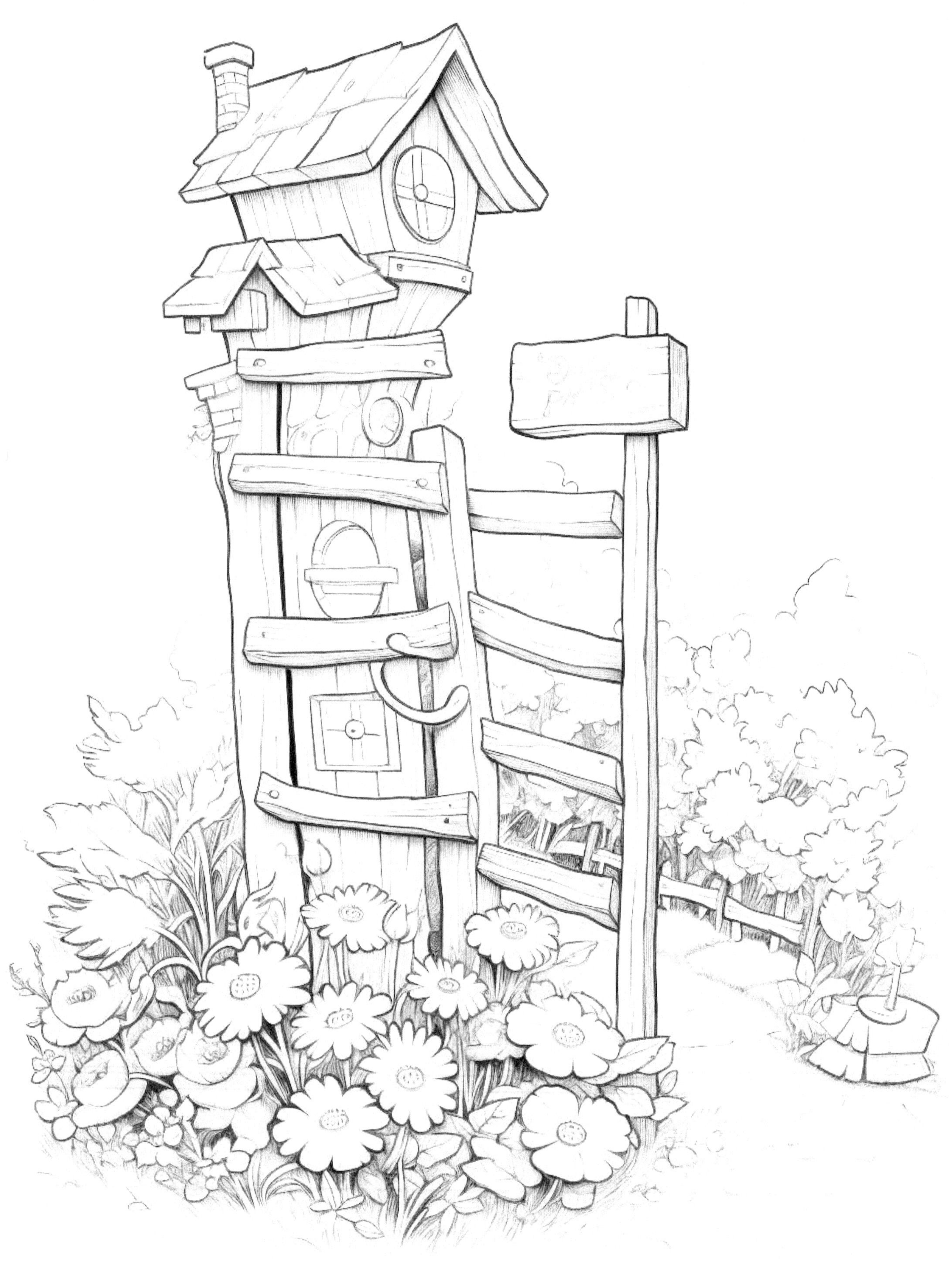

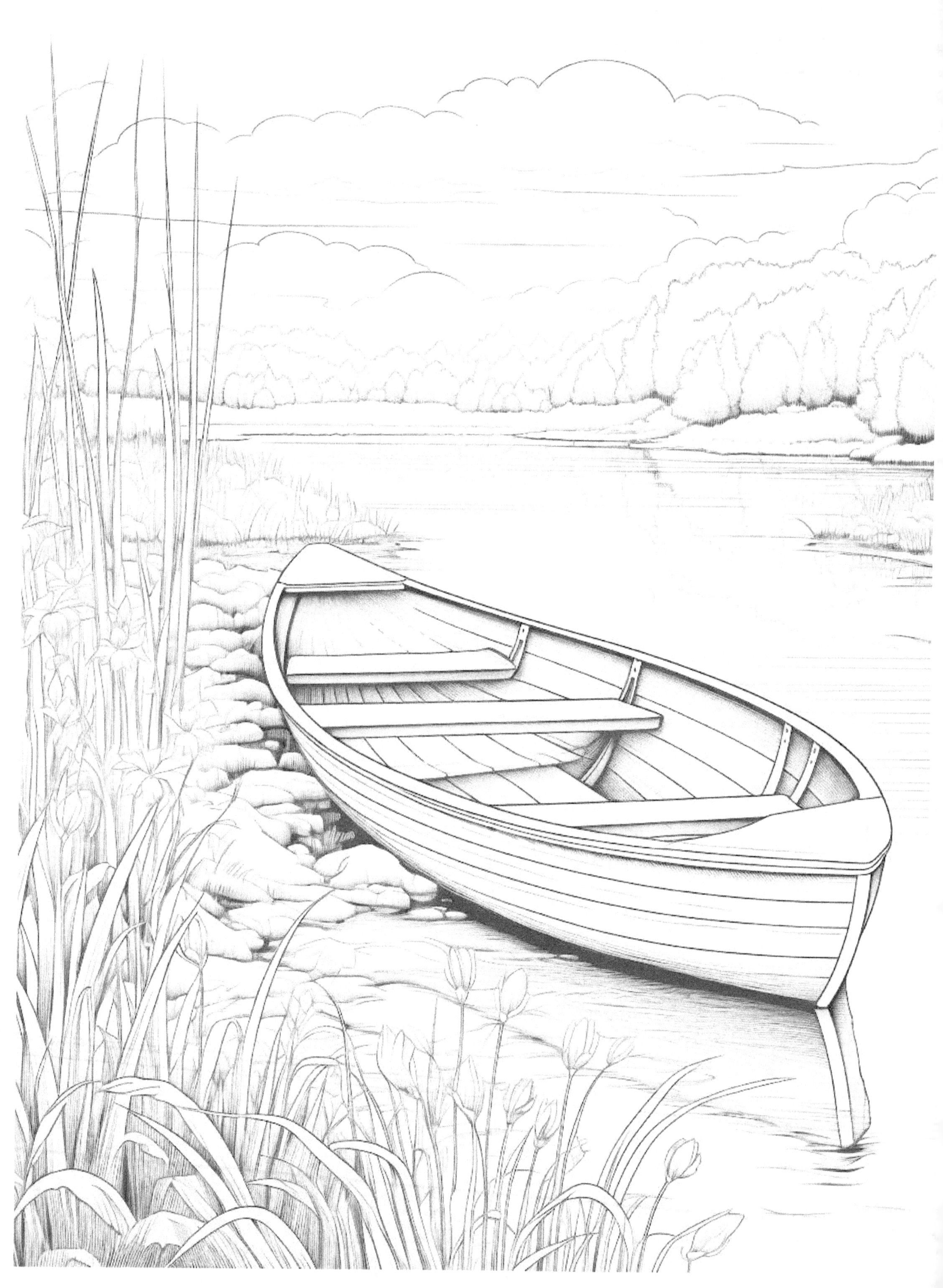

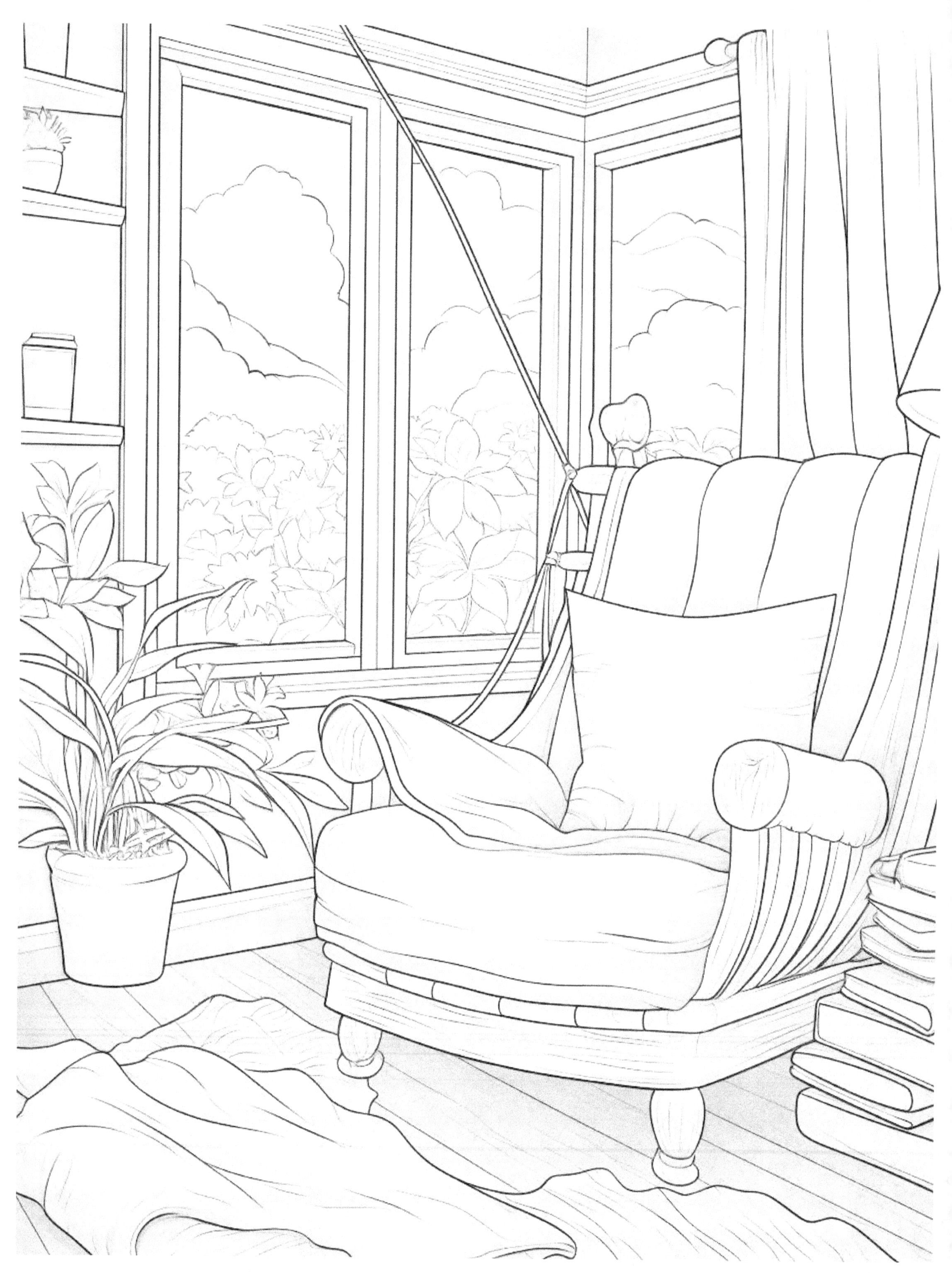

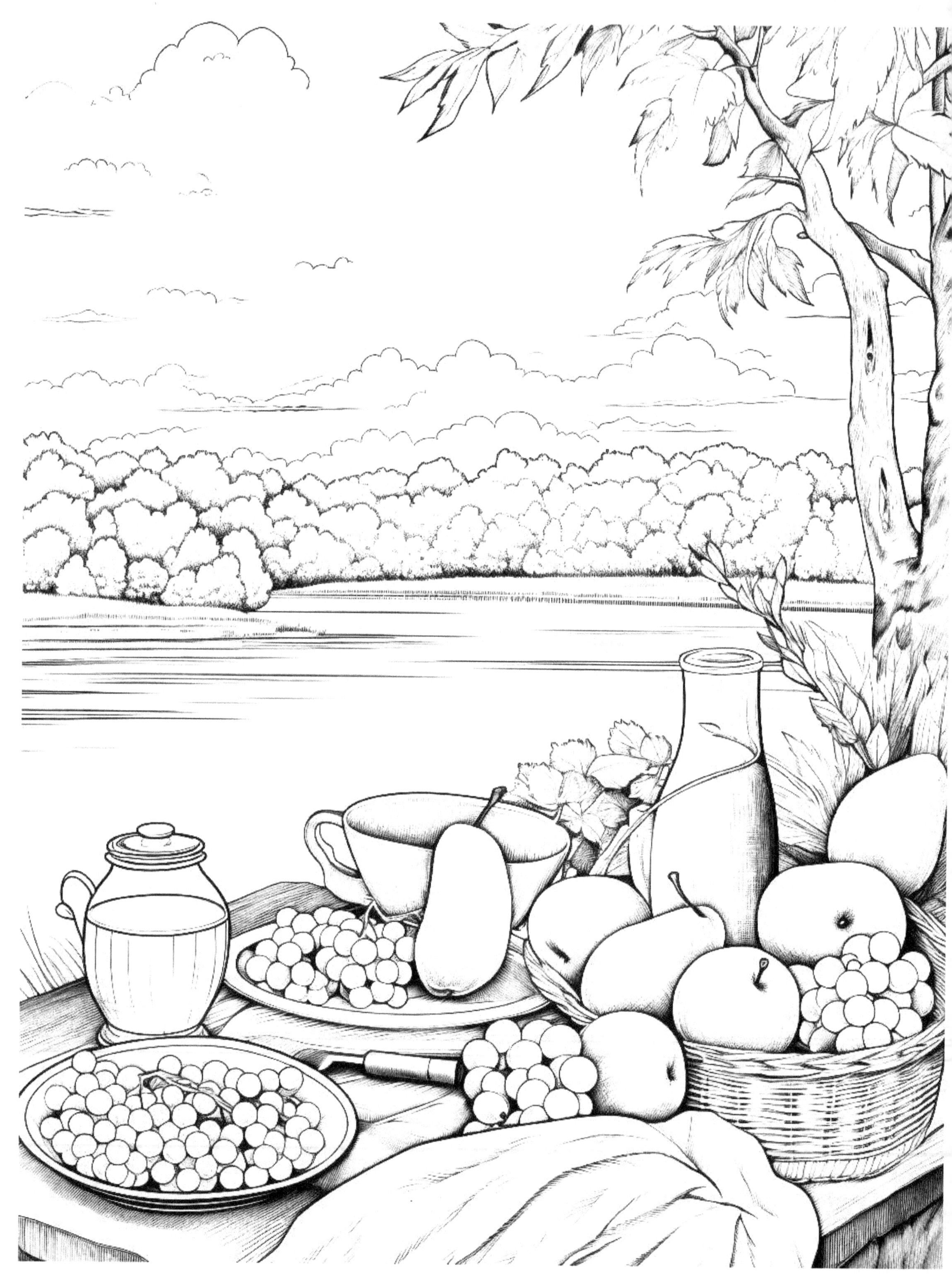

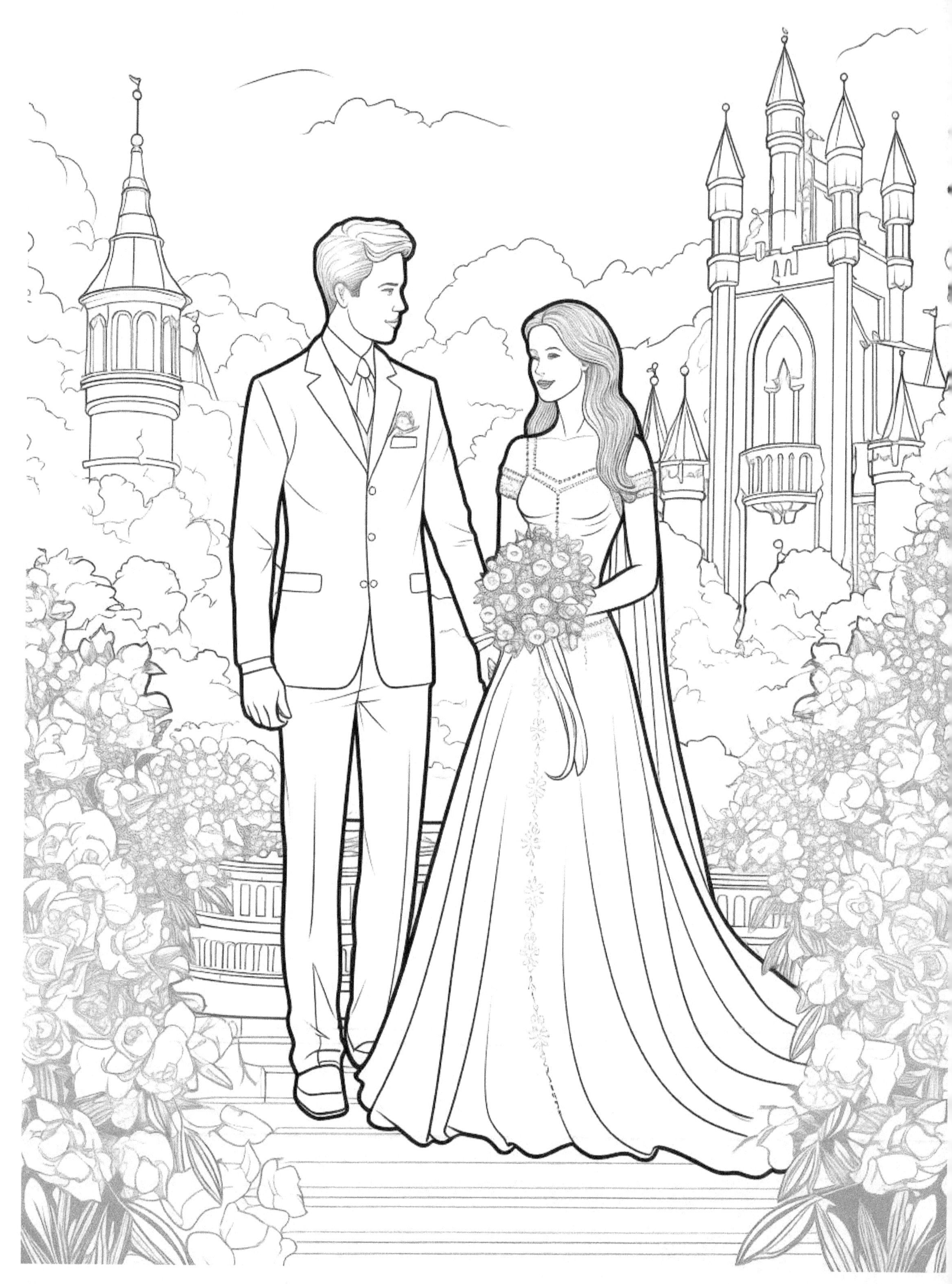

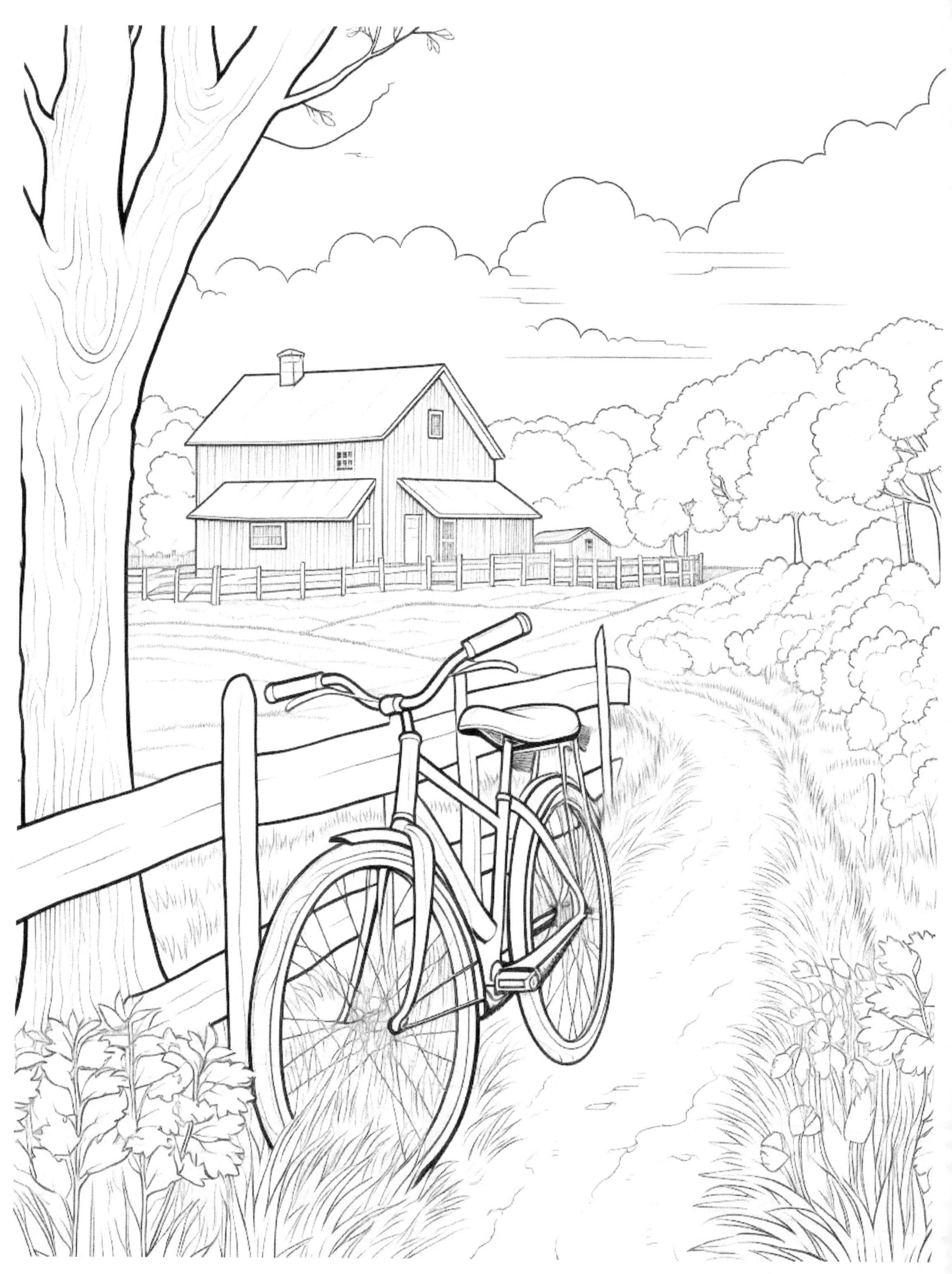

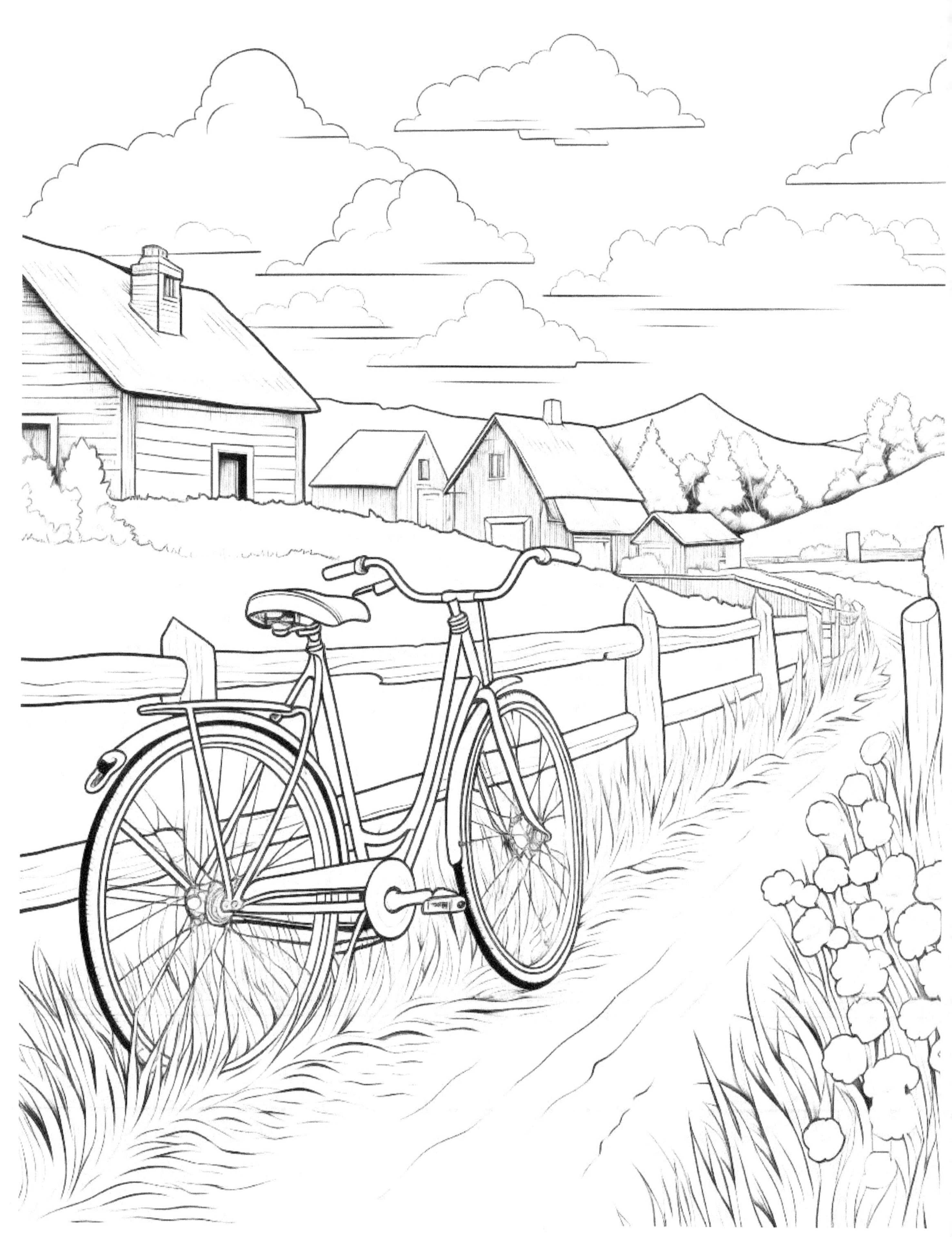

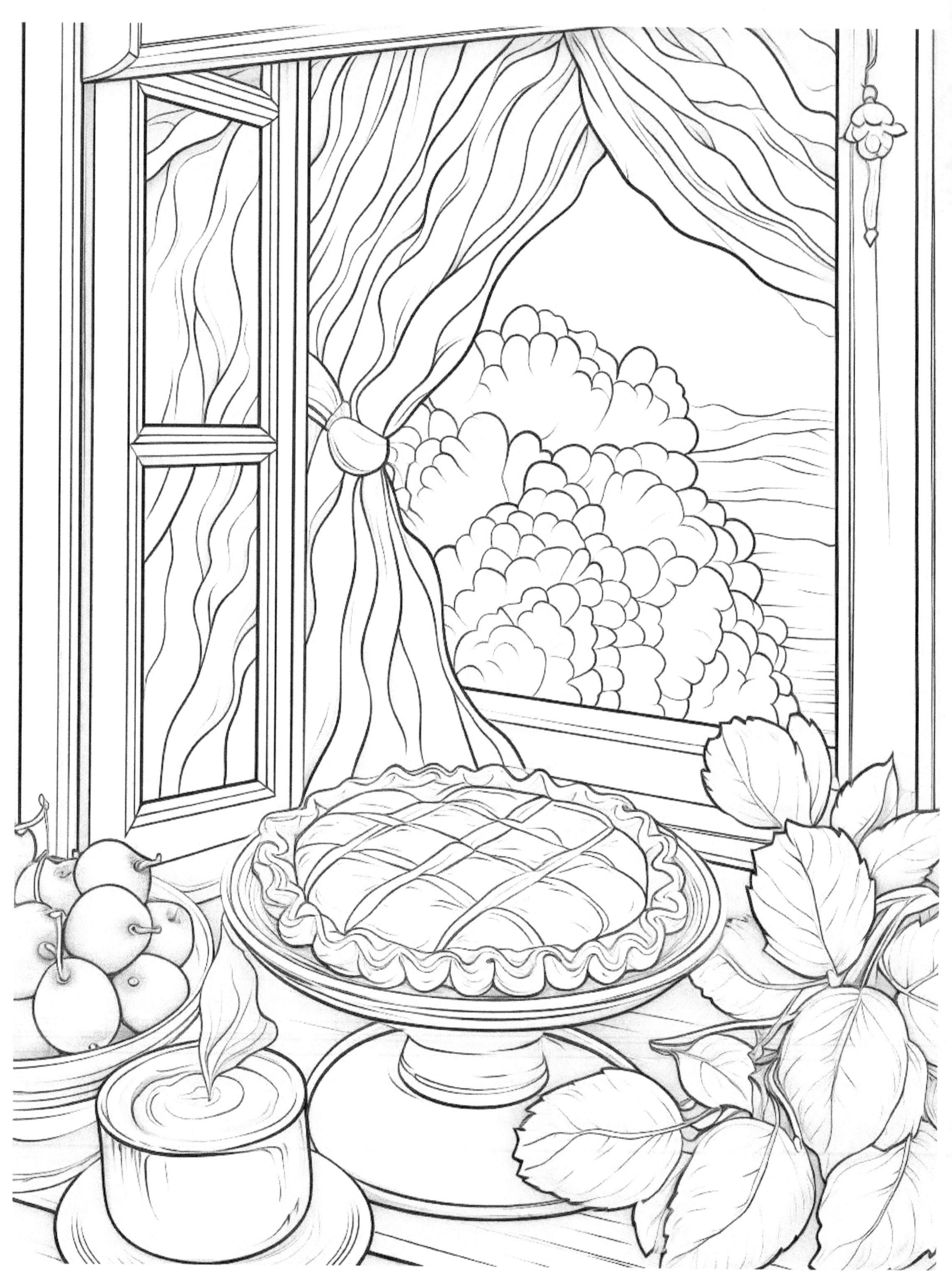

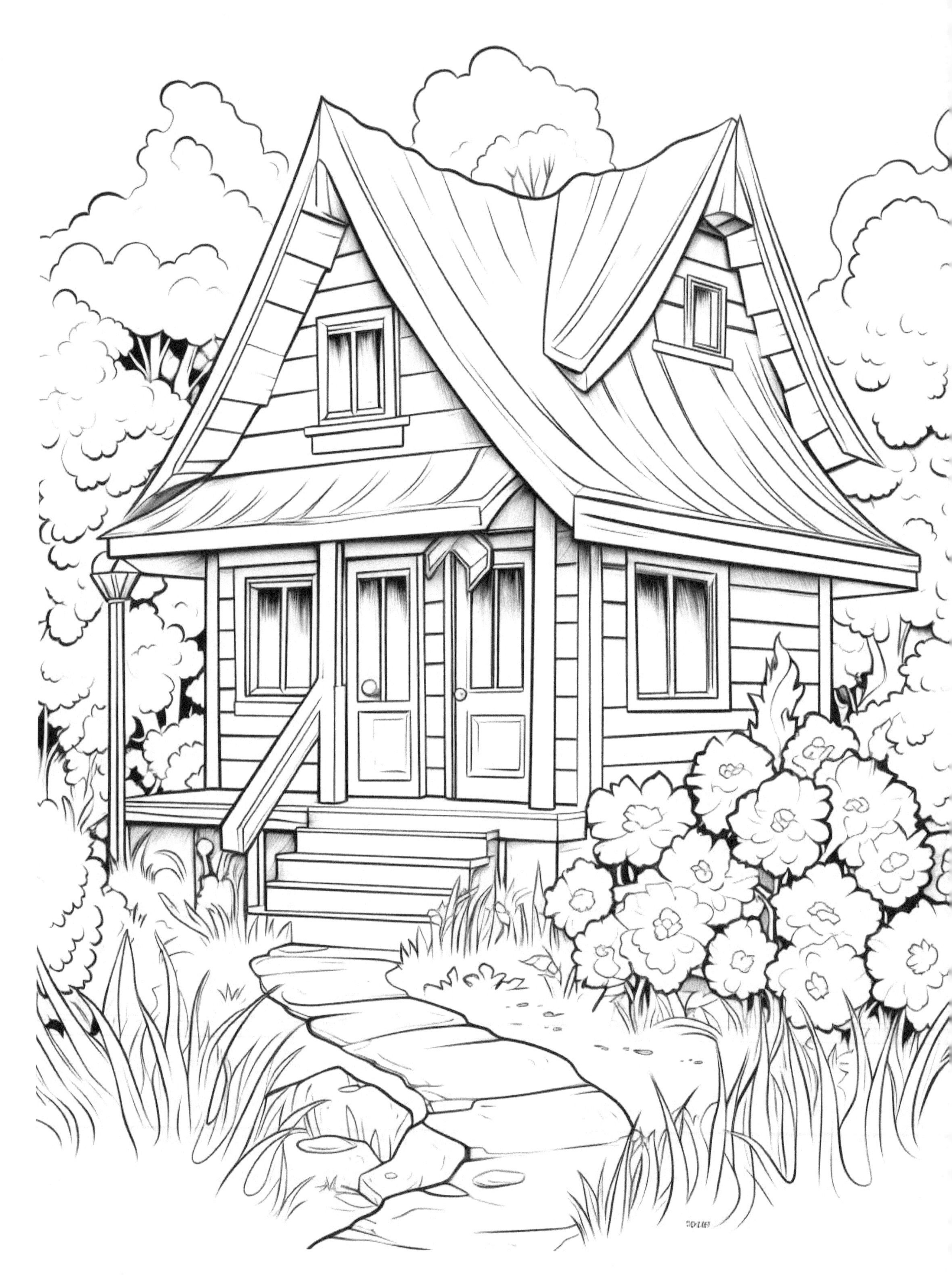

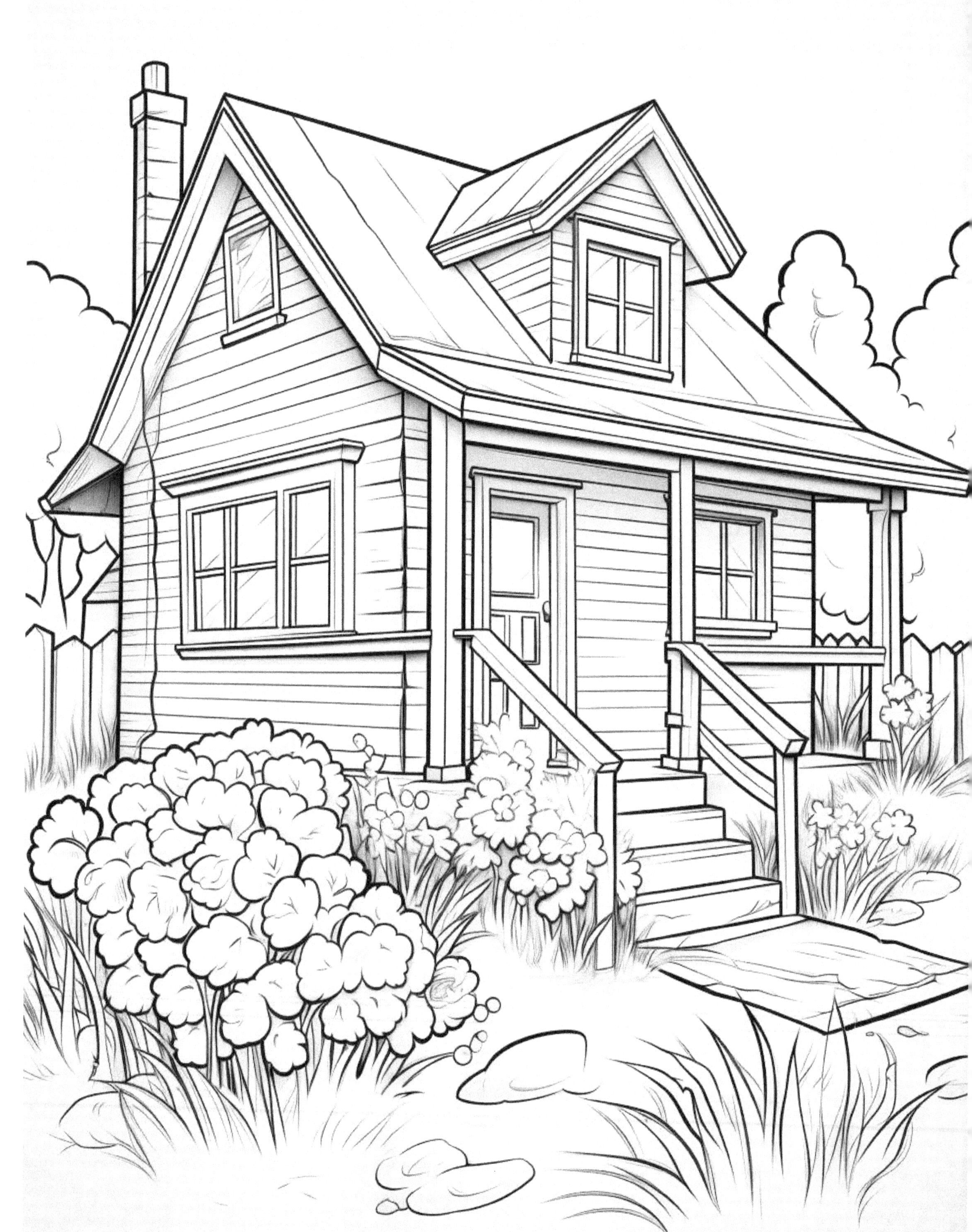

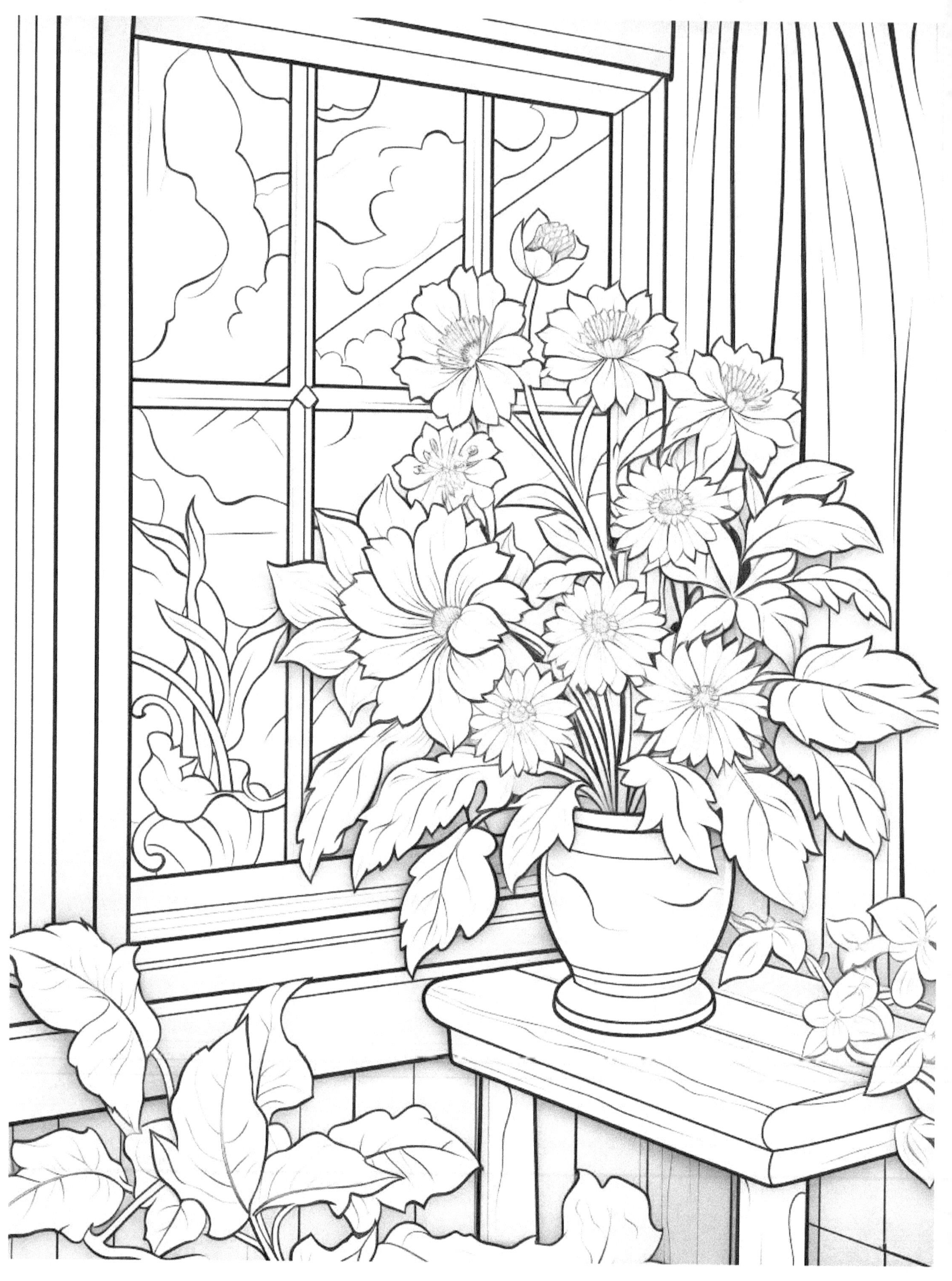

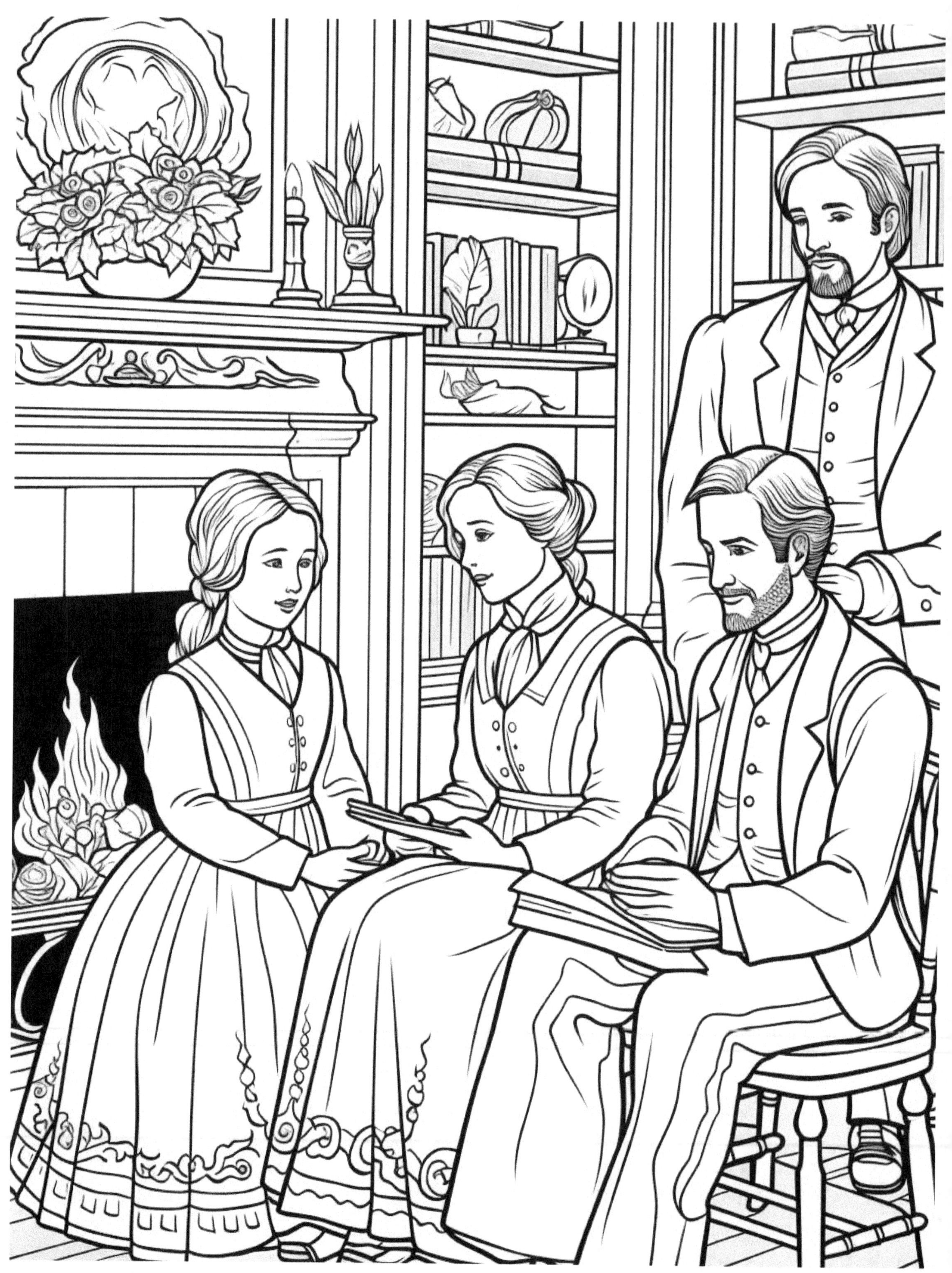

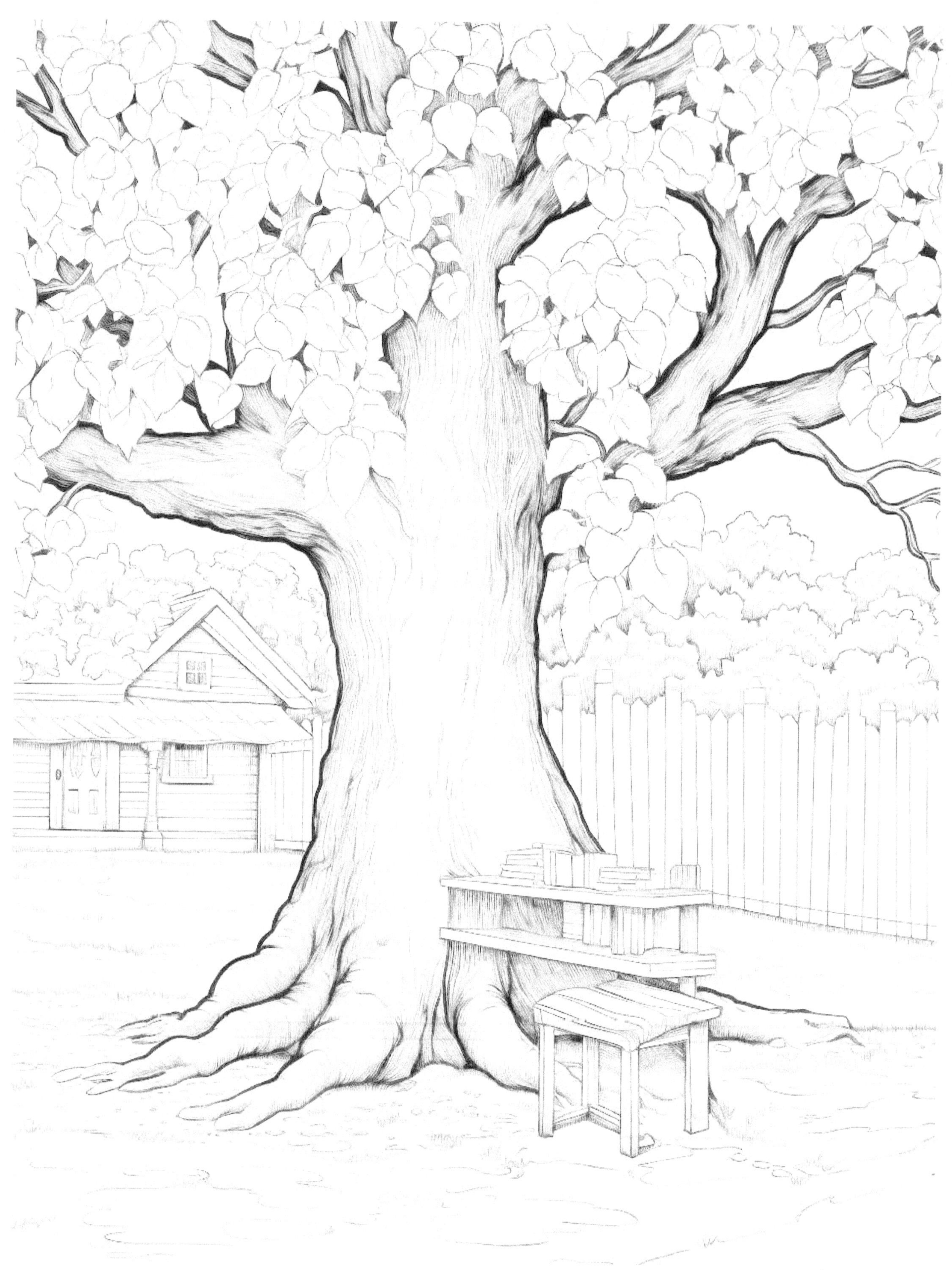

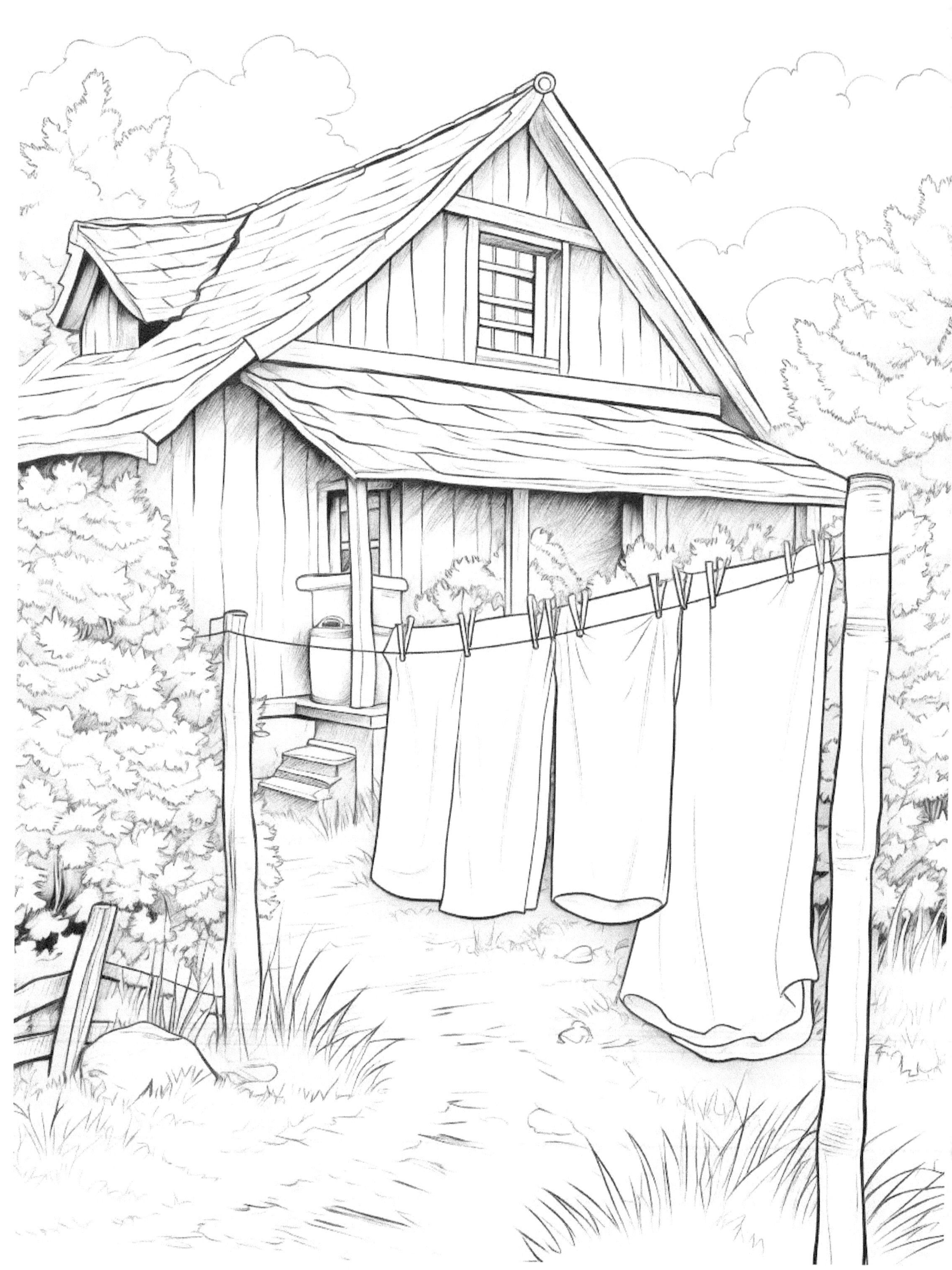

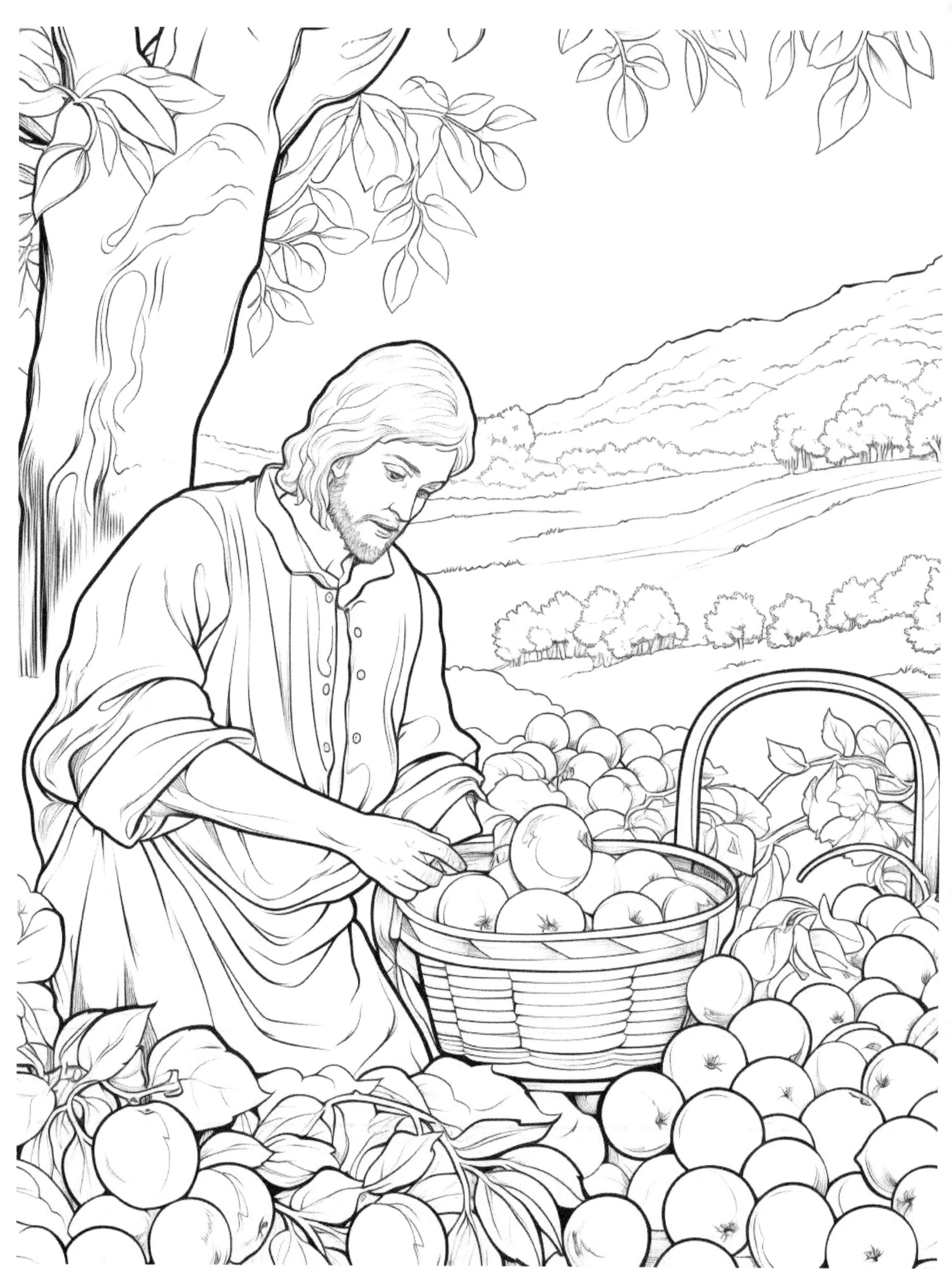

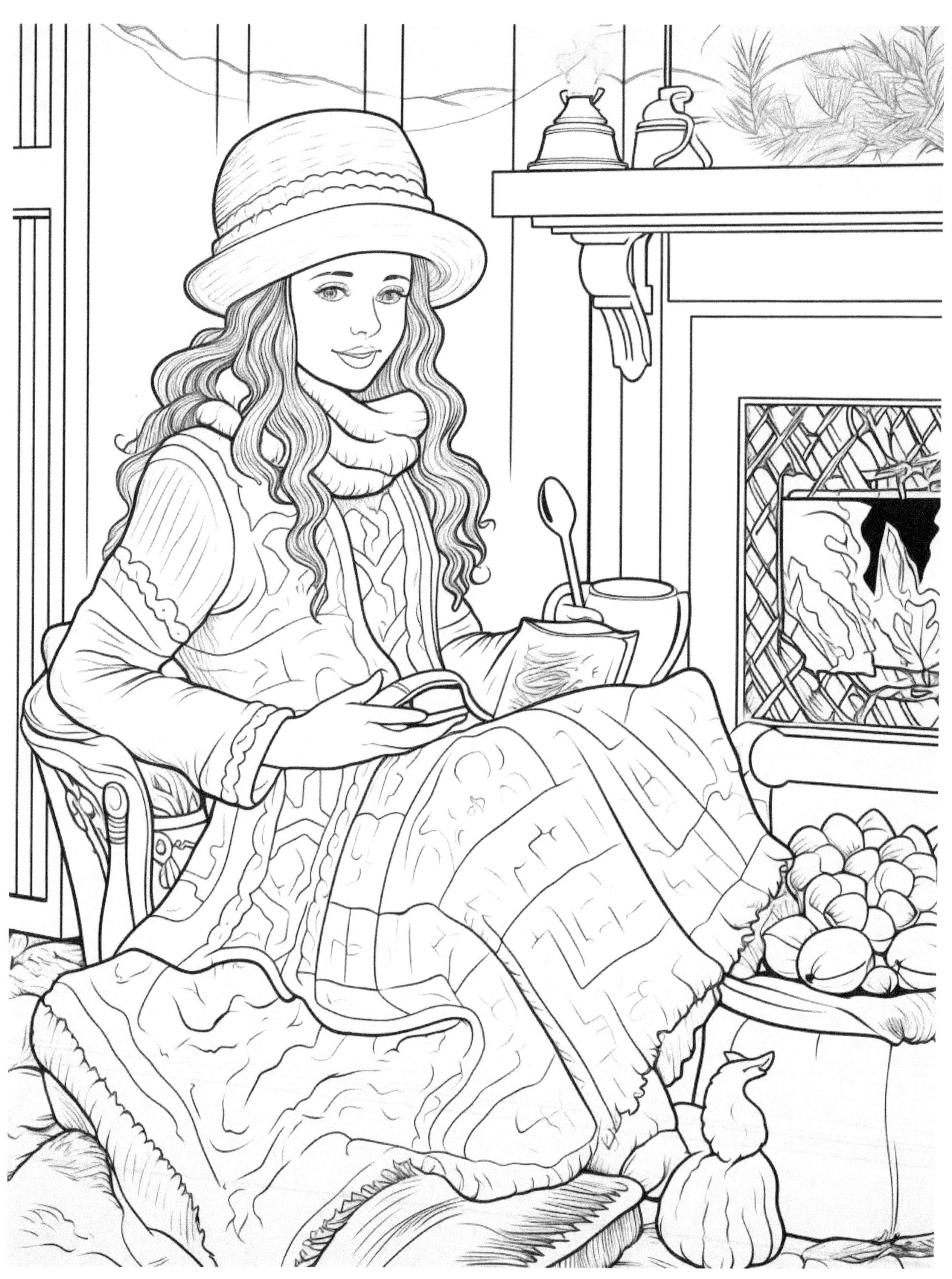

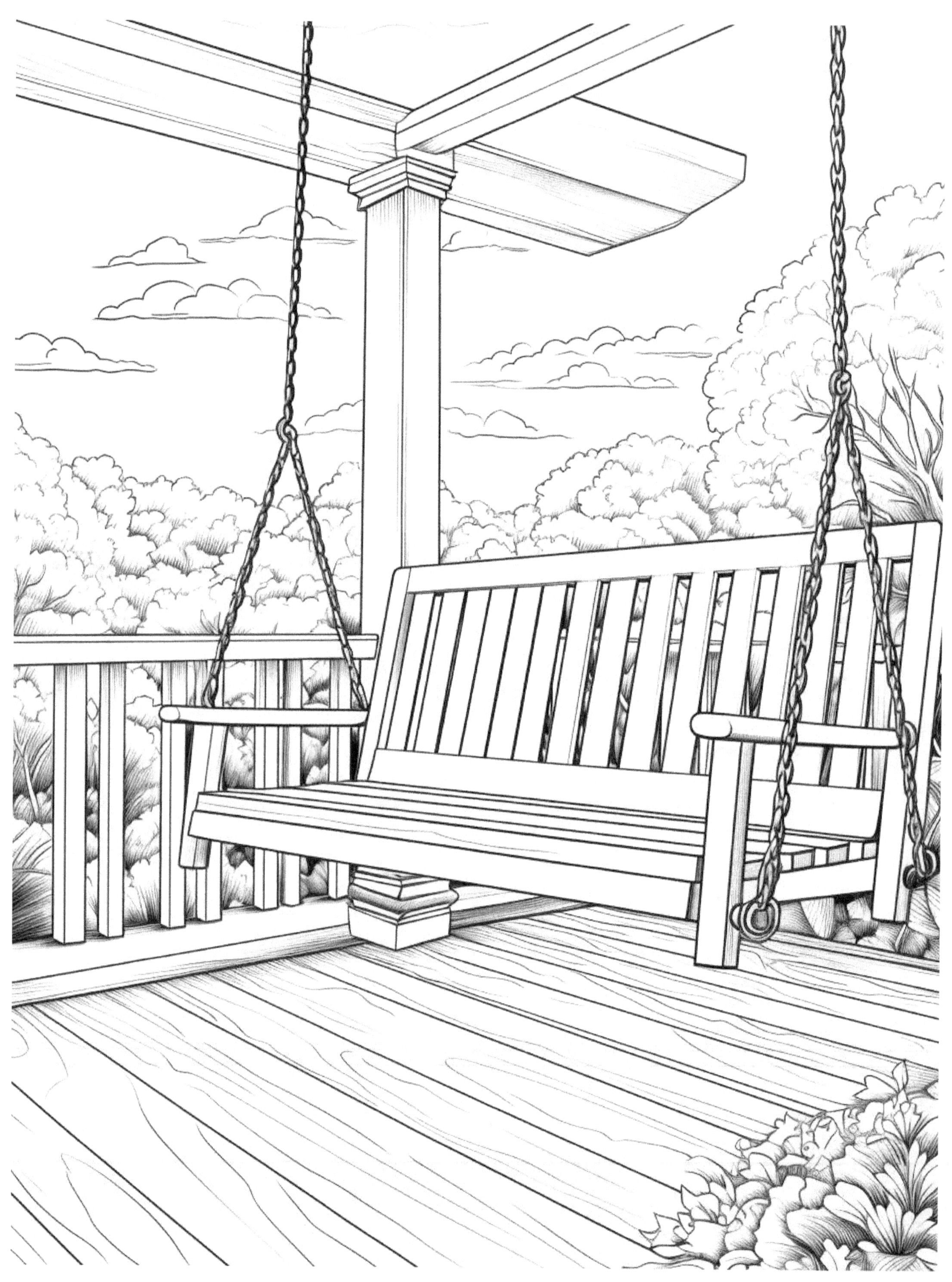

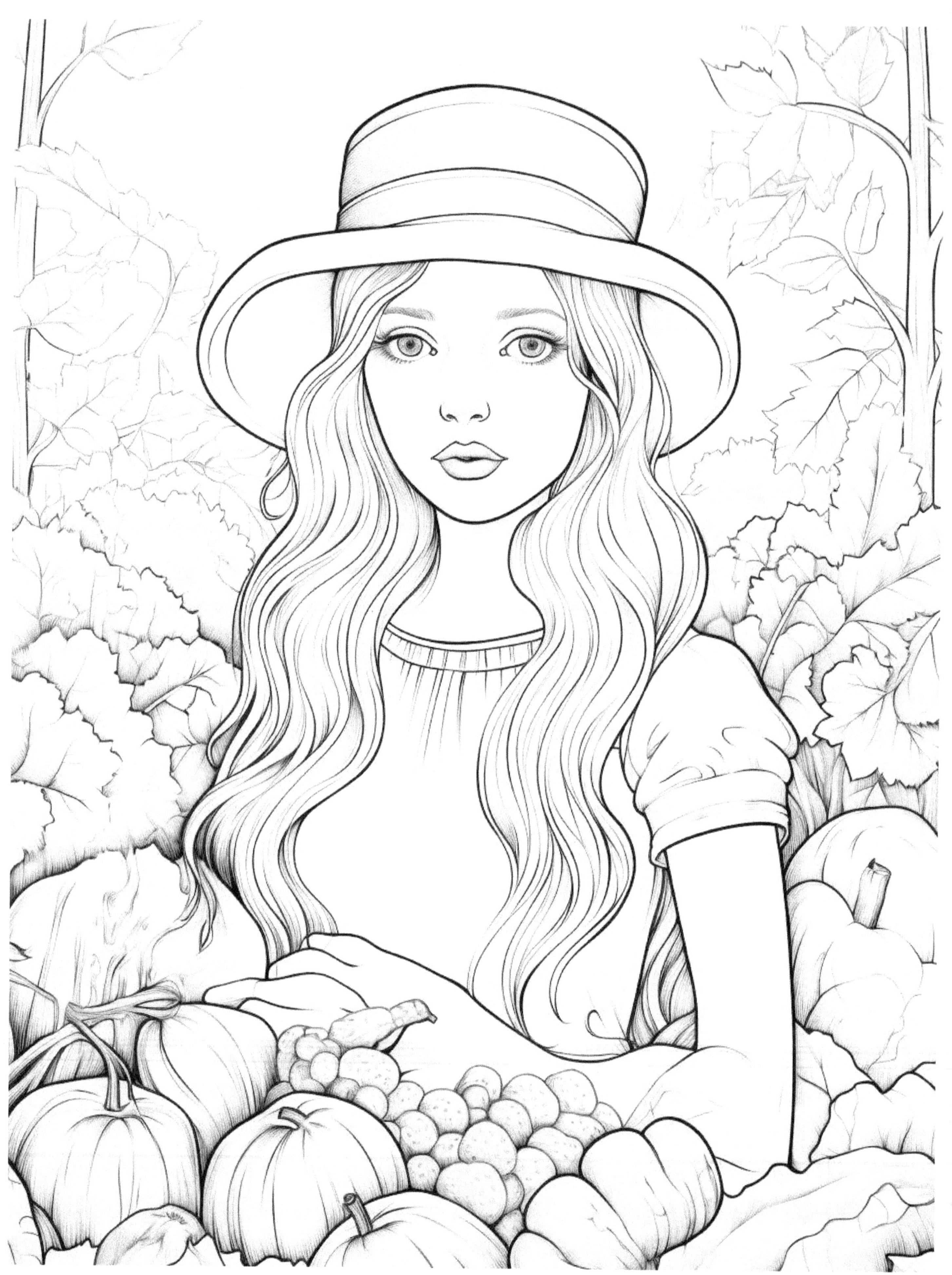

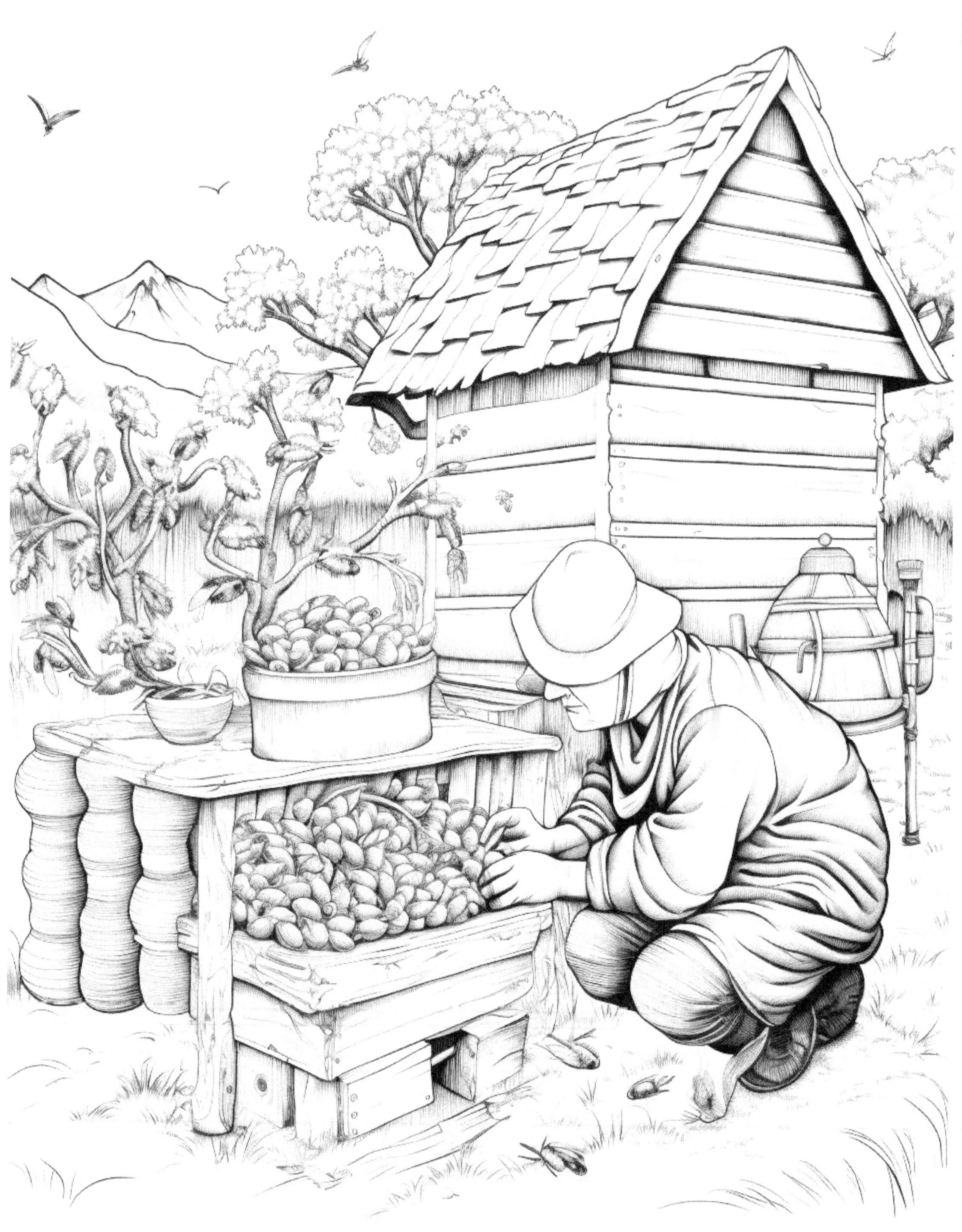

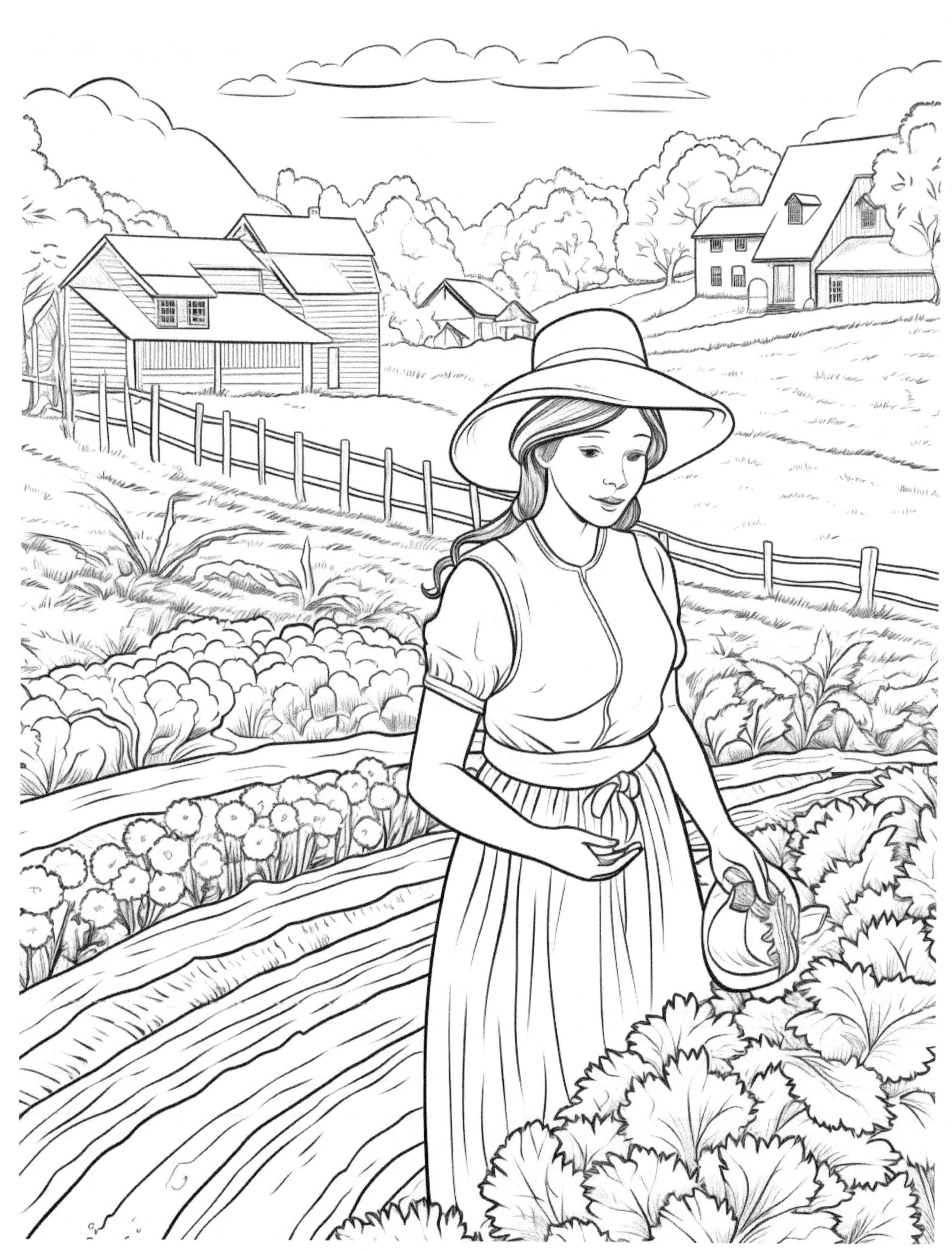

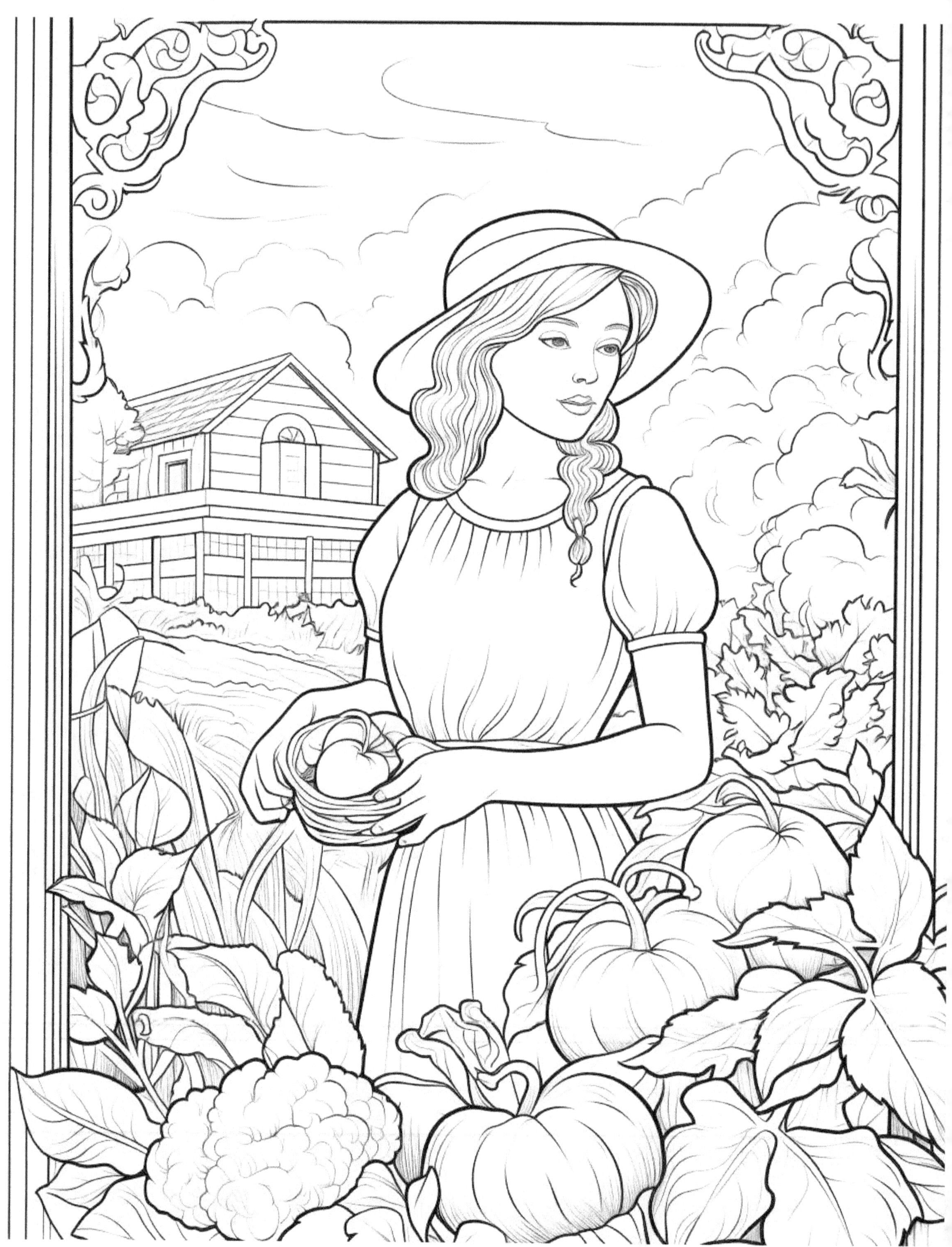